THE WORLD ACCORDING TO

THE WORLD ACCORDING TO

God

Selections from the
BOOK OF BOOKS
with the HOLY BIBLE,
New Living Translation

Lauren Marshay

PROMISE
PRESS
An Imprint of Barbour Publishing

Dedication

In memory of my dad, Rev. Johnie Banks Sr.,
my best friend, best critic, and
inspiration for the theme of this book.
To my mom, Willie Mae Banks,
a rare treasure and excellent role model.
I thank them for the love and guidance
they have given me throughout my life.
To my sister, Irma Banks,
for her steadfast prayers, love, encouragement, and input.
To my brother, Roy Banks, an author,
who inspired the idea to write a book.
To the rest of my family for their love and support.
And to Rev. Michael Hackbardt for his advice,
encouragement, and belief in the success of this book.

Contents

God

ALMIGHTY, CREATOR, REDEEMER, FATHER, SAVIOR, LORD

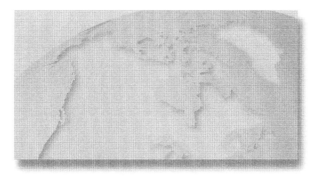

The Bible grows more beautiful
as we grow in our understanding of it.

—Johann Wolfgang von Goethe

In the beginning God created the heavens and the earth. God created people in his own image; male and female he created them. God blessed them and told them, "Multiply and fill the earth and subdue it. Be masters over the fish and birds and all the animals."

Genesis 1:1, 27–28

Christ is the one through whom God created everything in heaven and earth. He made the things we can see and the things we can't see—kings, kingdoms, rulers, and authorities. Everything has been created through him and for him. He existed before everything else began, and he holds all creation together.

Colossians 1:16–17

" 'You must love the Lord your God with all your heart, all your soul, and all your mind.' This is the first and greatest commandment."

Matthew 22:37–38

Acknowledge that the LORD is God! He made us, and we are his. We are his people, the sheep of his pasture. Enter his gates with thanksgiving; go into his courts with praise. Give thanks to him and bless his name. For the LORD is good. His unfailing love continues forever, and his faithfulness continues to each generation.

Psalm 100:3–5

I am the LORD; there is no other God. I have prepared you, even though you do not know me. . .I am the one who made the earth and created people to live on it. With my hands I stretched out the heavens. All the millions of stars are at my command. For the LORD is God, and he created the heavens and earth and put everything in place. He made the world to be lived in, not to be a place of empty chaos. "I am the LORD," he says, "and there is no other. I publicly proclaim bold promises. I do not whisper obscurities in some dark corner so no one can understand what I mean. And I did not tell the people of Israel to ask me for something I did not plan to give. I, the LORD, speak only what is true and right. Consult together, argue your case and state your proofs that idol worship pays. Who made these things known long ago? What idol ever told you they would happen? Was it not I, the LORD? For there is no other God but me—a just God and a Savior—no, not one! Let all the world look to me for salvation! For I am God; there is no other. I have sworn by my own name, and I will never go back on my word: Every knee will bow to me, and every tongue will confess allegiance to my name."

Isaiah 45:5, 12, 18–19, 21–23

So remember this and keep it firmly in mind: The LORD is God both in heaven and on earth, and there is no other god! If you obey all the laws and commands that I will give you today, all will be well with you and your children. Then you will enjoy a long life in the land the LORD your God is giving you for all time.

Deuteronomy 4:39–40

God is not a man, that he should lie. He is not a human, that he should change his mind. Has he ever spoken and failed to act? Has he ever promised and not carried it through?

Numbers 23:19

The LORD your God is the God of gods and Lord of lords. He is the great God, mighty and awesome, who shows no partiality and takes no bribes.

Deuteronomy 10:17

. . .

A single line in the Bible
has consoled me more than
all the books I have ever read.

Immanuel Kant

. . .

For the LORD your God is merciful—he will not abandon you or destroy you or forget the solemn covenant he made with your ancestors.

Deuteronomy 4:31

The LORD's promises are pure, like silver refined in a furnace, purified seven times over. As for God, his way is perfect. All the LORD's promises prove true. He is a shield for all who look to him for protection.

Psalm 12:6; 18:30

The LORD has made the heavens his throne; from there he rules over everything. But the LORD reigns forever, executing judgment from his throne. He will judge the world with justice and rule the nations with fairness.

Psalm 103:19; 9:7–8

The LORD is watching everywhere, keeping his eye on both the evil and the good. The LORD looks down from heaven and sees the whole human race. From his throne he observes all who live on the earth. He made their hearts, so he understands everything they do.

Proverbs 15:3; Psalm 33:13–15

. . .

We all long for heaven where God is,
but we have it in our power to be
in heaven with him right now—
to be happy with him at this very moment.

Mother Teresa of Calcutta

. . .

I will proclaim the name of the LORD; how glorious is our God! He is the Rock; his work is perfect. Everything he does is just and fair. He is a faithful God who does no wrong; how just and upright he is!

Deuteronomy 32:3–4

I know all the things you do, and I have opened a door for you that no one can shut. You have little strength, yet you obeyed my word and did not deny me. Can anyone hide from me? Am I not everywhere in all the heavens and earth? asks the LORD.

Revelation 3:8; Jeremiah 23:24

Praise the LORD; I tell myself; O LORD my God, how great you are! You are robed with honor and with majesty; you are dressed in a robe of light. You stretch out the starry curtain of the heavens; you lay out the rafters of your home in the rain clouds. You make the clouds your chariots; you ride upon the wings of the wind. You placed the world on its foundation so it would never be moved. You send rain on the mountains from your heavenly home, and you fill the earth with the fruit of your labor. You made the moon to mark the seasons and the sun that knows when to set. O LORD, what a variety of things you have made! In wisdom you have made them all. The earth is full of your creatures. May the glory of the LORD last forever! The LORD rejoices in all he has made! The LORD does whatever pleases him throughout all heaven and earth, and on the seas and in their depths.

Psalm 104:1–3, 5, 13, 19, 24, 31; 135:6

Great and marvelous are your actions, Lord God Almighty. Just and true are your ways, O King of the nations. Who will not fear, O Lord, and glorify your name? For you alone are holy. All nations will come and worship before you, for your righteous deeds have been revealed.

Revelation 15:3–4

Let the LORD's people show him reverence, for those who honor him will have all they need. Even strong young lions sometimes go hungry, but those who trust in the LORD will never lack any good thing.

Psalm 34:9–10

For the word of the LORD holds true, and everything he does is worthy of our trust. He loves whatever is just and good, and his unfailing love fills the earth. The LORD merely spoke, and the heavens were created. He breathed the word, and all the stars were born. Let everyone in the world fear the LORD, and let everyone stand in awe of him. For when he spoke, the world began! It appeared at his command.

Psalm 33:4–6, 8–9

Yours, O LORD, is the greatness, the power, the glory, the victory, and the majesty. Everything in the heavens and on earth is yours, O LORD, and this is your kingdom. We adore you as the one who is over all things. Riches and honor come from you alone, for you rule over everything. Power and might are in your hand, and it is at your discretion that people are made great and given strength.

I Chronicles 29:11–12

Praise the LORD! Praise God in his heavenly dwelling; praise him in his mighty heaven! Praise him for his mighty works; praise his unequaled greatness! Let everything that lives sing praises to the LORD! Praise the LORD!

Psalm 150:1–2, 6

*A thorough knowledge of
the Bible is worth
more than
a college education.*

—Theodore Roosevelt

For I am the LORD! What I threaten always happens. There will be no more delays, you rebels of Israel! I will fulfill my threat of destruction in your own lifetime, says the Sovereign LORD. It is the same with my word. I send it out, and it always produces fruit. It will accomplish all I want it to, and it will prosper everywhere I send it. Heaven and earth will disappear, but my words will remain forever.

Ezekiel 12:25; Isaiah 55:11; Matthew 24:35

. . .

Let nothing disturb thee,
Let nothing affright thee.
All things are passing.
God never changes.

Teresa of Avila

. . .

We work together as partners who belong to God. You are God's field, God's building—not ours. Don't you realize that all of you together are the temple of God and that the Spirit of God lives in you? So don't take pride in following a particular leader. Everything belongs to you: and you belong to Christ, and Christ belongs to God.

I Corinthians 3:9, 16, 21, 23

Forever, O LORD, your word stands firm in heaven. Your faithfulness extends to every generation, as enduring as the earth you created. Your laws remain true today, for everything serves your plans.

Psalm 119:89–91

Blessing and honor and glory and power belong to the one sitting on the throne and to the Lamb forever and ever. O LORD, our Lord, the majesty of your name fills the earth! Your glory is higher than the heavens.

Revelation 5:13; Psalm 8:1

Let every created thing give praise to the LORD, for he issued his command, and they came into being. He established them forever and forever. His orders will never be revoked. Let them all praise the name of the LORD. For his name is very great; his glory towers over the earth and heaven!

Psalm 148:5–6, 13

Great is the LORD! He is most worthy of praise! He is to be revered above all gods. The gods of other nations are merely idols, but the LORD made the heavens! Honor and majesty surround him; strength and beauty are in his dwelling. Give to the LORD the glory he deserves! Bring your offering and come to worship him.

1 Chronicles 16:25–27, 29

The LORD is righteous in everything he does; he is filled with kindness. The LORD is close to all who call on him, yes, to all who call on him sincerely. He fulfills the desires of those who fear him; he hears their cries for help and rescues them. The LORD protects all those who love him, but he destroys the wicked.

Psalm 145:17–20

Great is the LORD! He is most worthy of praise! His greatness is beyond discovery! Let each generation tell its children of your mighty acts. I will meditate on your majestic, glorious splendor and your wonderful miracles. The LORD is good to everyone. He showers compassion on all his creation. All of your works will thank you, LORD, and your faithful followers will bless you. For your kingdom is an everlasting kingdom. You rule generation after generation. The LORD is faithful in all he says; he is gracious in all he does.

Psalm 145:3–5, 9–10, 13

The earth is the LORD's, and everything in it. The world and all its people belong to him. For he laid the earth's foundation on the seas and built it on the ocean depths.

Psalm 24:1–2

God is mighty, yet he does not despise anyone! He is mighty in both power and understanding. Look, God is exalted beyond what we can understand. His years are without number.

Job 36:5, 26

Turn away from evil and do good. Work hard at living in peace with others. The eyes of the LORD watch over those who do right; his ears are open to their cries for help. But the LORD will redeem those who serve him. Everyone who trusts in him will be freely pardoned.

Psalm 34:14–15, 22

. . .

Born in the East and
clothed in Oriental form and imagery,
the Bible walks the ways of
all the world with familiar feet
and enters land after land to find its own everywhere.

Henry Van Dyke

. . .

Have you never heard or understood? Don't you know that the LORD is the everlasting God, the Creator of all the earth? He never grows faint or weary. No one can measure the depths of his understanding. "My thoughts are completely different from yours," says the LORD. "And my ways are far beyond anything you could imagine. For just as the heavens are higher than the earth, so are my ways higher than your ways, and my thoughts higher than your thoughts."

Isaiah 40:28; 55:8–9

But those who wait on the LORD will find new strength. They will fly high on wings like eagles. They will run and not grow weary. They will walk and not faint.

Isaiah 40:31

Don't be afraid, for I am with you. Do not be dismayed, for I am your God. I will strengthen you. I will help you. I will uphold you with my victorious right hand.

Isaiah 41:10

I see very clearly that God doesn't show partiality. In every nation he accepts those who fear him and do what is right. For the LORD God is our light and protector. He gives grace and glory. No good thing will the LORD withhold from those who do what is right. O LORD Almighty, happy are those who trust in you.

Acts 10:34–35; Psalm 84:11–12

Commit everything you do to the LORD. Trust him, and he will help you. He will make your innocence as clear as the dawn, and the justice of your cause will shine like the noonday sun. Be still in the presence of the LORD, and wait patiently for him to act. Don't worry about evil people who prosper or fret about their wicked schemes.

Psalm 37:5–7

O my people, trust in him at all times. Pour out your heart to him, for God is our refuge.

Psalm 62:8

Man's world has become a nervous one,
encompassed by anxiety.
God's world is other than this;
always balanced, calm,
and in order.

—Faith Baldwin

The Word

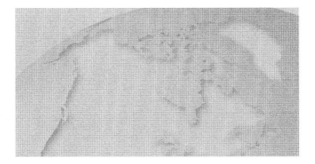

In the beginning the Word already existed. He was with God, and he was God. He was in the beginning with God. He created everything there is. Nothing exists that he didn't make. Life itself was in him, and this life gives light to everyone. The light shines through the darkness, and the darkness can never extinguish it.

John 1:1–5

All right then, the Lord himself will choose the sign. Look! The virgin will conceive a child. She will give birth to a son and will call him Immanuel— 'God is with us.' And she 'will have a son, and you are to name him Jesus, for he will save his people from their sins.

Isaiah 7:14; Matthew 1:21

In the sixth month of Elizabeth's pregnancy, God sent the angel Gabriel to Nazareth, a village in Galilee, to a virgin named Mary. She was engaged to be married to a man named Joseph, a descendant of King David. "Don't be frightened, Mary," the angel told her, "for God has decided to bless you! You will become pregnant and have a son, and you are to name him Jesus. He will be very great and will be called the Son of the Most High. And the Lord God will give him the throne of his ancestor David."

Luke 1:26–27, 30–32

There the child grew up healthy and strong. He was filled with wisdom beyond his years, and God placed his special favor upon him.

Luke 2:40

O love of God,
how deep and great.
Far deeper than man's deepest hate.

—Corrie ten Boom

Then Jesus, full of the Holy Spirit, left the Jordan River. He was led by the Spirit to go out into the wilderness, where the Devil tempted him for forty days. He ate nothing all that time and was very hungry. Then the Devil said to him, "If you are the Son of God, change this stone into a loaf of bread." But Jesus told him, "No! The Scriptures say, 'People need more than bread for their life.'" Then the Devil took him up and revealed to him all the kingdoms of the world in a moment of time. The Devil told him, "I will give you the glory of these kingdoms and authority over them—because they are mine to give to anyone I please. I will give it all to you if you will bow down and worship me." Jesus replied, "The Scriptures say, 'You must worship the Lord your God; serve only him.'" Then the Devil took him to Jerusalem, to the highest point of the Temple, and said, "If you are the Son of God, jump off! For the Scriptures say, 'He orders his angels to protect and guard you. And they will hold you with their hands to keep you from striking your foot on a stone.'" Jesus responded, "The Scriptures also say, 'Do not test the Lord your God.'" When the Devil had finished tempting Jesus, he left him until the next opportunity came. From then on, Jesus began to preach, "Turn from your sins and turn to God, because the Kingdom of Heaven is near."

Luke 4:1–13; Matthew 4:17

So the message about the Lord spread widely and had a powerful effect.

Acts 19:20

So the Word became human and lived here on earth among us. He was full of unfailing love and faithfulness. And we have seen his glory, the glory of the only Son of the Father. We have all benefitted from the rich blessings he brought to us—one gracious blessing after another. For the law was given through Moses; God's unfailing love and faithfulness came through Jesus Christ.

John 1:14, 16–17

After his baptism, as Jesus came up out of the water, the heavens were opened and he saw the Spirit of God descending like a dove and set-tling on him. . .and the Holy Spirit descended on him in the form of a dove. And a voice from heaven said, "You are my beloved son, and I am fully pleased with you."

Matthew 3:16; Luke 3:22

HEAD OF THE CHURCH

A man who was merely a man
and said the sort of things Jesus said
wouldn't be a great moral teacher.
He'd either be a lunatic—
on a level with a man who says
he's a poached egg—
or else he'd be the devil of hell.
You must make your choice.
Either this man was, and is,
the Son of God,
or else a madman or something worse.

—C. S. Lewis

For God so loved the world that he gave his only Son, so that everyone who believes in him will not perish but have eternal life.

John 3:16

And God has put all things under the authority of Christ, and he gave him this authority for the benefit of the church. And the church is his body; it is filled by Christ, who fills everything everywhere with his presence.

Ephesians 1:22–23

Christ is the visible image of the invisible God. He existed before God made anything at all and is supreme over all creation. Christ is the head of the church, which is his body. He is the first of all who will rise from the dead, so he is the first in everything. For God in all his fullness was pleased to live in Christ, and by him God reconciled everything to himself. He made peace with everything in heaven and on earth by means of his blood on the cross.

Colossians 1:15, 18–20

Christ is the head of his body, the church; he gave his life to be her Savior. He gave up his life for her. "I will build my church, and all the powers of hell will not conquer it. And I will give you the keys of the Kingdom of Heaven. Whatever you lock on earth will be locked in heaven, and whatever you open on earth will be opened in heaven."

Ephesians 5:23, 25; Matthew 16:18–19

"I am the light of the world. If you follow me, you won't be stumbling through the darkness, because you will have the light that leads to life."

John 8:12

"I am the way, the truth, and the life. No one can come to the Father except through me. However, those the Father has given me will come to me, and I will never reject them."

John 14:6; 6:37

"I am the bread of life. No one who comes to me will ever be hungry again. Those who believe in me will never thirst."

John 6:35

. . .

*I would rather walk with God
in the dark than go alone in the light.*

Mary Gardiner Brainard

. . .

"I am the living bread that came down out of heaven. Anyone who eats this bread will live forever; this bread is my flesh, offered so the world may live."

John 6:51

JESUS CHRIST:
HEAD OF THE CHURCH

"I am the gate for the sheep. Yes, I am the gate. Those who come in through me will be saved. Wherever they go, they will find green pastures."

John 10:7, 9

"I assure you, anyone who sneaks over the wall of a sheepfold, rather than going through the gate, must surely be a thief and a robber! For a shepherd enters through the gate. The gatekeeper opens the gate for him, and the sheep hear his voice and come to him. He calls his own sheep by name and leads them out. After he has gathered his own flock, he walks ahead of them, and they follow him because they recognize his voice. They won't follow a stranger; they will run from him because they don't recognize his voice."

John 10:1–5

"I am the true vine, and my Father is the gardener. Yes, I am the vine; you are the branches. Those who remain in me, and I in them, will produce much fruit. For apart from me you can do nothing. But if you stay joined to me and my words remain in you, you may ask any request you like, and it will be granted!"

John 15:1, 5, 7

"I am the resurrection and the life. Those who believe in me, even though they die like everyone else, will live again. They are given eternal life for believing in me and will never perish."

John 11:25–26

"I am the good shepherd. The good shepherd lays down his life for the sheep. I am the good shepherd; I know my own sheep, and they know me, just as my Father knows me and I know the Father. And I lay down my life for the sheep. The Father loves me because I lay down my life that I may have it back again. No one can take my life from me. I lay down my life voluntarily. For I have the right to lay it down when I want to and also the power to take it again. For my Father has given me this command."

John 10:11, 14–15, 17–18

. . .

All the armies that ever marched,
and all the navies that ever were built,
and all the parliaments that ever sat,
and all the kings that ever reigned, put together,
have not affected the life of man upon this earth
as powerfully as has this one solitary life.

Henry Benjamin Whipple

. . .

"See, I am coming soon, and my reward is with me, to repay all according to their deeds. I am the Alpha and the Omega, the First and the Last, the Beginning and the End."

Revelation 22:12–13

Because eternity
was closeted in time,
he is my open door
to forever.

—Luci Shaw

"I have come to you representing my Father, and you refuse to welcome me, even though you readily accept others who represent only themselves. For I have come down from heaven to do the will of God who sent me; not to do what I want. And this is the will of God, that I should not lose even one of all those he has given me, but that I should raise them to eternal life at the last day. For it is my Father's will that all who see his Son and believe in him should have eternal life—that I should raise them at the last day."

John 5:43; 6:38–40

"I am the Alpha and the Omega—the beginning and the end," says the Lord God. "I am the one who is, who always was, and who is still to come, the Almighty One. I am the First and the Last. I am the living one who died. Look, I am alive forever and ever! And I hold the keys of death and the grave."

Revelation 1:8, 17–18

"And I assure you that the time is coming, in fact it is here, when the dead will hear my voice—the voice of the Son of God. And those who listen will live. The Father has life in himself, and he has granted his Son to have life in himself. Don't be so surprised! Indeed, the time is coming when all the dead in their graves will hear the voice of God's Son, and they will rise again. Those who have done good will rise to eternal life, and those who have continued in evil will rise to judgment. I assure you, anyone who believes in me already has eternal life."

John 5:25–26, 28–29; 6:47

JESUS CHRIST:
HEAD OF THE CHURCH

HIS MINISTRY

Earth's crammed with heaven,
And every common bush afire with God;
But only he who sees, takes off his shoes—
The rest sit round it and pluck blackberries. . . .

—Elizabeth Barrett Browning

God did not send his Son into the world to condemn it, but to save it. There is no judgment awaiting those who trust him. But those who do not trust him have already been judged for not believing in the only Son of God.

John 3:17–18

"Healthy people don't need a doctor—sick people do. I have come to call sinners to turn from their sins, not to spend my time with those who think they are already good enough. My purpose is to give life in all its fullness."

Luke 5:31–32; John 10:10

"In the same way, heaven will be happier over one lost sinner who returns to God than over ninety-nine others who are righteous and haven't strayed away!"

Luke 15:7

"I assure you, those who listen to my message and believe in God who sent me have eternal life. They will never be condemned for their sins, but they have already passed from death into life."

John 5:24

"And I, the Son of Man, have come to seek and save those like him who are lost."

Luke 19:10

"Come to me, all of you who are weary and carry heavy burdens, and I will give you rest. Take my yoke upon you. Let me teach you, because I am humble and gentle, and you will find rest for your souls. For my yoke fits perfectly and the burden I give you is light."

Matthew 11:28–30

. . .

He paints the wayside flower,
He lights the evening star.

Jane Montgomery Campbell

. . .

"So if the Son sets you free, you will indeed be free." So Christ has really set us free. Now make sure that you stay free, and don't get tied up again in slavery to the law.

John 8:36; Galatians 5:1

"The Spirit of the Lord is upon me, for he has appointed me to preach Good News to the poor. He has sent me to proclaim that captives will be released, that the blind will see, that the downtrodden will be freed from their oppressors, and that the time of the Lord's favor has come. This Scripture has come true today before your very eyes!"

Luke 4:18–19, 21

This is what he taught them:

"God blesses those who realize their need for him, for the Kingdom of Heaven is given to them.

"God blesses those who mourn, for they will be comforted.

"God blesses those who are gentle and lowly, for the whole earth will belong to them.

"God blesses those who are hungry and thirsty for justice, for they will receive it in full.

"God blesses those who are merciful, for they will be shown mercy.

"God blesses those whose hearts are pure, for they will see God.

"God blesses those who work for peace, for they will be called the children of God.

"God blesses those who are persecuted because they live for God, for the Kingdom of Heaven is theirs.

"God blesses you when you are mocked and persecuted and lied about because you are my followers. Be happy about it! Be very glad! For a great reward awaits you in heaven. And remember, the ancient prophets were persecuted, too."

Matthew 5:2–12

"In that way, you will be acting as true children of your Father in heaven. For he gives his sunlight to both the evil and the good, and he sends rain on the just and on the unjust, too. But you are to be perfect, even as your Father in heaven is perfect."

Matthew 5:45, 48

"Stop judging others, and you will not be judged. Stop criticizing others, or it will all come back on you. If you forgive others, you will be forgiven."

Luke 6:37

. . .

Christ's life outwardly was one of
the most troubled lives that was ever lived:
tempest and tumult, tumult and tempest,
the waves breaking over it all the time.
But the inner life was a sea of glass.
The great calm was always there.

Henry Drummond

. . .

"For others will treat you as you treat them. Whatever measure you use in judging others, it will be used to measure how you are judged. And why worry about a speck in your friend's eye when you have a log in your own? How can you think of saying, 'Friend, let me help you get rid of that speck in your eye,' when you can't see past the log in your own eye? Hypocrite! First get rid of the log from your own eye; then perhaps you will see well enough to deal with the speck in your friend's eye."

Matthew 7:2–5

JESUS CHRIST:
HIS MINISTRY

"But if you are willing to listen, I say, love your enemies. Do good to those who hate you. Pray for the happiness of those who curse you. Pray for those who hurt you. If someone slaps you on one cheek, turn the other cheek. If someone demands your coat, offer your shirt also. Give what you have to anyone who asks you for it; and when things are taken away from you, don't try to get them back. Do for others as you would like them to do for you.

"Do you think you deserve credit merely for loving those who love you? Even the sinners do that! And if you do good only to those who do good to you, is that so wonderful? Even sinners do that much! And if you lend money only to those who can repay you, what good is that? Even sinners will lend to their own kind for a full return.

"Love your enemies! Do good to them! Lend to them! And don't be concerned that they might not repay. Then your reward from heaven will be very great, and you will truly be acting as children of the Most High, for he is kind to the unthankful and to those who are wicked. You must be compassionate, just as your Father is compassionate."

Luke 6:27–36

HE BEGAN TO TEACH THE PEOPLE BY TELLING MANY STORIES SUCH AS THIS ONE:

Story of the Farmer Scattering Seed

"Listen! A farmer went out to plant some seed. As he scattered it across his field, some seed fell on a footpath, and the birds came and ate it. Other seed fell on shallow soil with underlying rock. The plant sprang up quickly, but it soon wilted beneath the hot sun and died because the roots had no nourishment in the shallow soil. Other seed fell among thorns that shot up and choked out the tender blades so that it produced no grain. Still other seed fell on fertile soil and produced a crop that was thirty, sixty, and even a hundred times as much as had been planted." Then he said, "Anyone who is willing to hear should listen and understand!"

Mark 4:2–9

His disciples asked him what the story meant.

Luke 8:9

"But if you can't understand this story, how will you understand all the others I am going to tell? The farmer I talked about is the one who brings God's message to others. The seed that fell on the hard path represents those who hear the message, but then Satan comes at once and takes it away from them. The rocky soil represents those who hear the message and receive it with joy. But like young plants in such soil, their roots don't go very deep. At first they get along fine, but they wilt as soon as they have problems or are persecuted because they believe the word. The thorny ground represents those who hear and accept the Good News, but all too quickly the message is crowded out by the cares of this life, the lure of wealth, and the desire for nice things, so no crop is produced. But the good soil represents those who hear and accept God's message and produce a huge harvest—thirty, sixty, or even a hundred times as much as had been planted."

Mark 4:13–20

*Jesus is God
spelling himself out in language
that man can understand.*

—Samuel Dickey Gordon

"Anyone who is willing to hear should listen and understand! To those who are open to my teaching, more understanding will be given. But to those who are not listening, even what they have will be taken away from them."

Mark 4:23, 25

HERE IS ANOTHER STORY JESUS TOLD:

Story of the Wheat and Weeds

"The Kingdom of Heaven is like a farmer who planted good seed in his field. But that night as everyone slept, his enemy came and planted weeds among the wheat. When the crop began to grow and produce grain, the weeds also grew. The farmer's servants came and told him, 'Sir, the field where you planted that good seed is full of weeds!'

" 'An enemy has done it!' the farmer exclaimed!

" 'Shall we pull out the weeds?' they asked.

"He replied, 'No, you'll hurt the wheat if you do. Let both grow together until the harvest. Then I will tell the harvesters to sort out the weeds and burn them and to put the wheat in the barn.' "

Matthew 13:24–30

JESUS CHRIST:
HIS MINISTRY

"Please explain the story of the weeds in the field."

"All right," he said. "I, the Son of Man, am the farmer who plants the good seed. The field is the world, and the good seed represents the people of the Kingdom. The weeds are the people who belong to the evil one. The enemy who planted the weeds among the wheat is the Devil. The harvest is the end of the world, and the harvesters are the angels.

"Just as the weeds are separated out and burned, so it will be at the end of the world. I, the Son of Man, will send my angels, and they will remove from my Kingdom everything that causes sin and all who do evil, and they will throw them into the furnace and burn them. There will be weeping and gnashing of teeth. Then the godly will shine like the sun in their Father's Kingdom. Anyone who is willing to hear should listen and understand!"

Matthew 13:36–43

"Here is another illustration of what the Kingdom of God is like: A farmer planted seeds in a field, and then he went on with his other activities. As the days went by, the seeds sprouted and grew without the farmer's help, because the earth produces crops on its own. First a leaf blade pushes through, then the heads of wheat are formed, and finally the grain ripens. And as soon as the grain is ready, the farmer comes and harvests it with a sickle."

Mark 4:26–29

"Mr. Webster, can you comprehend how Jesus Christ could be both God and man?"
No sir, I cannot comprehend it;
and I would be ashamed to acknowledge him
as my Savior if I could comprehend it.
If I could comprehend him,
he could be no greater than myself,
and such is my conviction
of accountability to God,
such is my sense of sinfulness before him,
and such is my knowledge of
my own incapacity to recover myself,
that I feel I need a superhuman Savior.

—Daniel Webster

Story of the Three Servants

"Again, the Kingdom of Heaven can be illustrated by the story of a man going on a trip. He called together his servants and gave them money to invest for him while he was gone. He gave five bags of gold to one, two bags of gold to another, and one bag of gold to the last—dividing it in proportion to their abilities—and then left on his trip. The servant who received the five bags of gold began immediately to invest the money and soon doubled it. The servant with two bags of gold also went right to work and doubled the money. But the servant who received the one bag of gold dug a hole in the ground and hid the master's money for safekeeping.

"After a long time their master returned from his trip and called them to give an account of how they had used his money. The servant to whom he had entrusted the five bags of gold said, 'Sir, you gave me five bags of gold to invest, I have doubled the amount.' The master was full of praise. 'Well done, my good and faithful servant. You have been faithful in handling this small amount, so now I will give you many more responsibilities. Let's celebrate together!'

"Next came the servant who had received the two bags of gold, with the report, 'Sir, you gave me two bags of gold to invest, and I have doubled the amount.' The master said, 'Well done, my good and faithful servant. You have been faithful in handling this small amount, so now I will give you many more responsibilities. Let's celebrate together!'

"Then the servant with the one bag of gold came and said, 'Sir, I know you are a hard man, harvesting crops you didn't plant and gathering crops you didn't cultivate. I was afraid I would lose your money, so I hid it in the earth and here it is.'

"But the master replied, 'You wicked and lazy servant! You think I'm a hard man, do you, harvesting crops I didn't plant and gathering crops I didn't cultivate? Well, you should at least have put my money into the bank so I could have some interest. Take the money from this servant and give it to the one with the ten bags of gold. Now throw this useless servant into outer darkness, where there will be weeping and gnashing of teeth.'"

Matthew 25:14–28, 30

"The coming of the Son of Man can be compared with that of a man who left home to go on a trip. He gave each of his employees instructions about the work they were to do, and he told the gatekeeper to watch for his return. So keep a sharp lookout! For you do not know when the homeowner will return—at evening, midnight, early dawn, or late daybreak. Don't let him find you sleeping when he arrives without warning. What I say to you, I say to everyone: Watch for his return!"

Mark 13:34–37

"At last the time has come! . . . The Kingdom of God is near! Turn from your sins and believe this Good News!"

Mark 1:15

Story of the Fig Tree

"Now, learn a lesson from the fig tree. When its buds become tender and its leaves begin to sprout, you know without being told that summer is near."

Mark 13:28

THEN JESUS USED THIS ILLUSTRATION:

"A man planted a fig tree in his garden and came again and again to see if there was any fruit on it, but he was always disappointed. Finally, he said to his gardener, 'I've waited three years, and there hasn't been a single fig! Cut it down. It's taking up space we can use for something else.'

"The gardener answered, 'Give it one more chance. Leave it another year, and I'll give it special attention and plenty of fertilizer. If we get figs next year, fine. If not, you can cut it down.'"

Luke 13:6–9

"Notice the fig tree, or any other tree. When the leaves come out, you know without being told that summer is near. Just so, when you see the events I've described taking place, you can be sure that the Kingdom of God is near.'"

Luke 21:29–31

"Don't let anyone mislead you, because many will come in my name, claiming to be the Messiah. They will lead many astray."

Mark 13:5–6

. . .

I saw a stable, low and very bare.
The oxen knew him, had him in their care.
To me he was a stranger.
The safety of the world was lying there
And the world's danger.

Mary Coleridge

. . .

"Beware of false prophets who come disguised as harmless sheep, but are really wolves that will tear you apart. You can detect them by the way they act, just as you can identify a tree by its fruit. You don't pick grapes from thornbushes, or figs from thistles. A healthy tree produces good fruit, and an unhealthy tree produces bad fruit. A good tree can't produce bad fruit, and a bad tree can't produce good fruit. So every tree that does not produce good fruit is chopped down and thrown into the fire. Yes, the way to identify a tree or a person is by the kind of fruit that is produced."

Matthew 7:15–20

Dear friends, do not believe everyone who claims to speak by the Spirit. You must test them to see if the spirit they have comes from God. For there are many false prophets in the world. This is the way to find out if they have the Spirit of God: If a prophet acknowledges that Jesus Christ became a human being, that person has the Spirit of God. If a prophet does not acknowledge Jesus, that person is not from God. Such a person has the spirit of the Antichrist. You have heard that he is going to come into the world, and he is already here.

1 John 4:1–3

"So if someone tells you, 'Look, the Messiah is out in the desert,' don't bother to go and look. Or, 'Look, he is hiding here,' don't believe it! For as the lightning lights up the entire sky, so it will be when the Son of Man comes. Immediately after those horrible days end, the sun will be darkened, the moon will not give light, the stars will fall from the sky, and the powers of heaven will be shaken. And then at last, the sign of the coming of the Son of Man will appear in the heavens, and there will be deep mourning among all the nations of the earth. And they will see the Son of Man arrive on the clouds of heaven with power and great glory. And he will send forth his angels with the sound of a mighty trumpet blast, and they will gather together his chosen ones from the farthest ends of the earth and heaven.

"Now learn a lesson from the fig tree. When its buds become tender and its leaves begin to sprout, you know without being told that summer is near. Just so, when you see the events I've described beginning to happen, you can know his return is very near, right at the door."

Matthew 24:26–27, 29–33

To the dead he sayeth: Arise!
To the living: Follow me!
And that voice still soundeth on
From the centuries that are gone,
To the centuries that shall be!

—Henry Wadsworth Longfellow

"Check their predictions against my testimony," says the LORD. "If their predictions are different from mine, it is because there is no light or truth in them."

Isaiah 8:20

"And then if anyone tells you, 'Look, here is the Messiah,' or, 'There he is,' don't pay any attention. For false messiahs and false prophets will rise up and perform miraculous signs and wonders so as to deceive, if possible, even God's chosen ones."

Mark 13:21–22

In the last days, God said, I will pour out my Spirit upon all people. Your sons and daughters will prophesy, your young men will see visions, and your old men will dream dreams.

And I will cause wonders in the heavens above and signs on the earth below—blood and fire and clouds of smoke. The sun will be turned into darkness, and the moon will turn blood red, before that great and glorious day of the Lord arrives. And anyone who calls on the name of the Lord will be saved.

Acts 2:17, 19–21

"You are truly my disciples if you keep obeying my teachings. And you will know the truth, and the truth will set you free.

"I assure you that everyone who sins is a slave of sin. A slave is not a permanent member of the family, but a son is part of the family forever. So if the Son sets you free, you will indeed be free."

John 8:31–32, 34–36

"I assure you, this generation will not pass from the scene until all these events have taken place. Heaven and earth will disappear, but my words will remain forever.

"Watch out! Don't let me find you living in careless ease and drunkenness, and filled with the worries of this life. Don't let that day catch you unaware, as in a trap. For that day will come upon everyone living on the earth. Keep a constant watch. And pray that, if possible, you may escape these horrors and stand before the Son of Man."

Luke 21:32–36

You should also know this, . . .that in the last days there will be very difficult times. For people will love only themselves and their money. They will be boastful and proud, scoffing at God, disobedient to their parents, and ungrateful. They will consider nothing sacred. They will be unloving and unforgiving; they will slander others and have no self-control; they will be cruel and have no interest in what is good. They will betray their friends, be reckless, be puffed up with pride, and love pleasure rather than God. They will act as if they are religious, but they will reject the power that could make them godly. You must stay away from people like that.

They are the kind who work their way into people's homes and win the confidence of vulnerable women who are burdened with the guilt of sin and controlled by many desires. Such women are forever following new teachings, but they never understand the truth.

2 Timothy 3:1–7

JESUS CHRIST:
HIS MINISTRY

"And wars will break out near and far, but don't panic. Yes, these things must come, but the end won't follow immediately. The nations and kingdoms will proclaim war against each other, and there will be famines and earthquakes in many parts of the world. But all this will be only the beginning of the horrors to come.

"Then you will be arrested, persecuted, and killed. You will be hated all over the world because of your allegiance to me. And many false prophets will appear and will lead many people astray. But those who endure to the end will be saved.

"For that will be a time of greater horror than anything the world has ever seen or will ever see again."

Matthew 24:6–9, 11, 13, 21

. . .

Only a step to Jesus!
Believe, and thou shalt live:
Lovingly now he's waiting.
And ready to forgive.

Fanny Crosby

. . .

Story of the Ten Bridesmaids

"Not all people who sound religious are really godly. They may refer to me as 'Lord,' but they still won't enter the Kingdom of Heaven. The decisive issue is whether they obey my Father in heaven. On judgment day many will tell me, 'Lord, Lord, we prophesied in your name and cast out demons in your name and performed many miracles in your name.' But I will reply, 'I never knew you. Go away; the things you did were unauthorized.'

"Anyone who listens to my teaching and obeys me is wise, like a person who builds a house on solid rock. Though the rain comes in torrents and the floodwaters rise and the winds beat against the house, it won't collapse, because it is built on rock. But anyone who hears my teaching and ignores it is foolish, like a person who builds a house on sand. When the rains and floods come and the winds beat against that house, it will fall with a mighty crash."

Matthew 7:21–27

"But when the head of the house has locked the door, it will be too late. Then you will stand outside knocking and pleading, 'Lord, open the door for us!' But he will reply, 'I do not know you.' You will say, 'But we ate and drank with you, and you taught in our streets.' And he will reply, 'I tell you. I don't know you. Go away, all you who do evil.'

"And there will be great weeping and gnashing of teeth, for you will see Abraham, Isaac, Jacob, and all the prophets within the Kingdom of God, but you will be thrown out."

Luke 13:25–28

JESUS CHRIST:
HIS MINISTRY

"The Kingdom of Heaven can be illustrated by the story of ten brides-maids who took their lamps and went to meet the bridegroom. Five of them were foolish, and five were wise. The five who were foolish took no oil for their lamps, but the other five were wise enough to take along extra oil. When the bridegroom was delayed, they all lay down and slept. At midnight they were roused by the shout, 'Look, the bride-groom is coming! Come out and welcome him!'

"All the bridesmaids got up and prepared their lamps. Then the five foolish ones asked the others, 'Please give us some of your oil because our lamps are going out.' But the others replied, 'We don't have enough for all of us. Go to a shop and buy some for yourselves.'

"But while they were gone to buy oil, the bridegroom came, and those who were ready went in with him to the marriage feast, and the door was locked. Later, when the other five bridesmaids returned, they stood outside, calling, 'Sir, open the door for us!' But he called back, 'I don't know you!' "

Matthew 25:1–12

Not only do we know God
through Jesus Christ,
we only know ourselves
through Jesus Christ.

—Blaise Pascal

Story of the Great Feast

"The Kingdom of Heaven can be illustrated by the story of a king who prepared a great wedding feast for his son. Many guests were invited, and when the banquet was ready, he sent his servants to notify everyone that it was time to come. But they all refused! So he sent other servants to tell them, 'The feast has been prepared, and choice meats have been cooked. Everything is ready. Hurry!' But the guests he had invited ignored them and went about their business, one to his farm, another to his store. Others seized his messengers and treated them shamefully, even killing some of them.

"Then the king became furious. He sent out his army to destroy the murderers and burn their city. And he said to his servants, 'The wedding feast is ready, and the guests I invited aren't worthy of the honor. Now go out to the street corners and invite everyone you see.'

"So the servants brought in everyone they could find, good and bad alike, and the banquet hall was filled with guests. But when the king came in to meet the guests, he noticed a man who wasn't wearing the proper clothes for a wedding. 'Friend,' he asked, 'how is it that you are here without wedding clothes?' And the man had no reply. Then the king said to his aides, 'Bind him hand and foot and throw him out into the outer darkness, where there is weeping and gnashing of teeth.' For many are called, but few are chosen."

Matthew 22:1–14

I know very well how foolish the message of the cross sounds to those who are on the road to destruction. But we who are being saved recognize this message as the very power of God.

I Corinthians 1:18

. . .

Nor can we fall below the arms of God,
how lowsoever it be we fall.

William Penn

. . .

"Blessed are those who are invited to the wedding feast of the Lamb."

Revelation 19:9

Story of the Unforgiving Debtor

Then Peter came to him and asked, "Lord, how often should I forgive someone who sins against me? Seven times?"

"No!" Jesus replied, "seventy times seven!"

"For this reason, the Kingdom of Heaven can be compared to a king who decided to bring his accounts up to date with servants who had borrowed money from him. In the process, one of his debtors was brought in who owed him millions of dollars. He couldn't pay, so the king ordered that he, his wife, his children, and everything he had be sold to pay the debt. But the man fell down before the king and begged him. 'Oh, sir, be patient with me, and I will pay it all.' Then the king was filled with pity for him, and he released him and forgave his debt.

"But when the man left the king, he went to a fellow servant who owed him a few thousand dollars. He grabbed him by the throat and demanded instant payment. His fellow servant fell down before him and begged for a little more time. 'Be patient and I will pay it,' he pleaded. But his creditor wouldn't wait. He had the man arrested and jailed until the debt could be paid in full.

"When some of the other servants saw this, they were very upset. They went to the king and told him what had happened. Then the king called in the man he had forgiven and said, 'You evil servant! I forgave you that tremendous debt because you pleaded with me. Shouldn't you have mercy on your fellow servant, just as I had mercy on you?' Then the angry king sent the man to prison until he had paid every penny.

"That's what my heavenly Father will do to you if you refuse to forgive your brothers and sisters in your heart."

Matthew 18:21–35

Centuries of experience have tested the Bible.
It has passed through critical fires
no other volume has suffered,
and its spiritual truth has endured the flames
and come out without so much
a the smell of burning.

—W. E. Sangster

Story of the Good Samaritan

One day an expert in religious law stood up to test Jesus by asking him this question: "Teacher, what must I do to receive eternal life?"

Jesus replied, "What does the law of Moses say? How do you read it?"

The man answered, " 'You must love the Lord your God with all your heart, all your soul, all your strength, and all your mind.' And, 'Love your neighbor as yourself.' "

"Right!" Jesus told him. "Do this and you will live."

The man wanted to justify his actions, so he asked Jesus, "And who is my neighbor?"

Jesus replied with an illustration: "A Jewish man was traveling on a trip from Jerusalem to Jericho, and he was attacked by bandits. They stripped him of his clothes and money, beat him up, and left him half dead beside the road.

"By chance, a Jewish priest came along; but when he saw the man lying there, he crossed to the other side of the road and passed him by. A Temple assistant walked over and looked at him lying there, but he also passed by on the other side.

"Then a despised Samaritan came along, and when he saw the man, he felt deep pity. Kneeling beside him, the Samaritan soothed his wounds with medicine and bandaged them. Then he put the man on his own donkey and took him to an inn, where he took care of him. The next day he handed the innkeeper two pieces of silver, and told him to take care of the man. 'If his bill runs higher than that,' he said, 'I'll pay the difference the next time I am here.'

"Now which of these three would you say was a neighbor to the man who was attacked by bandits?" Jesus asked.

The man replied, "The one who showed him mercy."

Then Jesus said, "Yes, now go and do the same."

Luke 10:25–37

Jesus Heals Many

Two blind men followed along behind him, shouting, "Son of David, have mercy on us!"

They went right into the house where he was staying, and Jesus asked them, "Do you believe I can make you see?"

"Yes, Lord," they told him, "we do."

Then he touched their eyes and said, "Because of your faith, it will happen." And suddenly they could see!

Matthew 9:27–30

Then a demon-possessed man, who was both blind and unable to talk, was brought to Jesus. He healed the man so that he could both speak and see. The crowd was amazed. "Could it be that Jesus is the Son of David, the Messiah?"

Matthew 12:22–23

They had come to hear him and to be healed, and Jesus cast out many evil spirits. Everyone was trying to touch him, because healing power went out from him, and they were all cured.

Luke 6:18–19

The hardness of God is
kinder than the softness of men,
and his compulsion is
our liberation.

—C. S. Lewis

He saw a woman who had been crippled by an evil spirit. She had been bent double for eighteen years and was unable to stand up straight. When Jesus saw her, he called her over and said, "Woman, you are healed of your sickness!" Then he touched her, and instantly she could stand straight. How she praised and thanked God!

Luke 13:11–13

A woman who had had a hemorrhage for twelve years came up behind him. She touched the fringe of his robe, for she thought, "If I can just touch his robe, I will be healed."

Jesus turned around and said to her, "Daughter, be encouraged! Your faith has made you well." And the woman was healed at that moment.

Matthew 9:20–22

Immediately the bleeding stopped, and she could feel that she had been healed!

Mark 5:29

That evening at sunset, many sick and demon-possessed people were brought to Jesus. So Jesus healed great numbers of sick people who had many different kinds of diseases, and he ordered many demons to come out of their victims.

Mark 1:32, 34

One day while Jesus was teaching, some Pharisees and teachers of religious law were sitting nearby. (It seemed that these men showed up from every village in all Galilee and Judea, as well as from Jerusalem.) And the Lord's healing power was strongly with Jesus. Some men came carrying a paralyzed man on a sleeping mat. They tried to push through the crowd to Jesus, but they couldn't reach him. So they went up to the roof, took off some tiles, and lowered the sick man down into the crowd, still on his mat, right in front of Jesus. Seeing their faith, Jesus said to the man, "Son, your sins are forgiven."

"Who does this man think he is?" the Pharisees and teachers of religious law said to each other. "This is blasphemy! Who but God can forgive sins?"

Jesus knew what they were thinking, so he asked them, "Why do you think this is blasphemy? Is it easier to say, 'Your sins are forgiven,' or 'Get up and walk?' I will prove that I, the Son of Man, have the authority on earth to forgive sins. Then Jesus turned to the paralyzed man and said, 'Stand up, take your mat, and go on home, because you are healed!'

And immediately, as everyone watched, the man jumped to his feet, picked up his mat, and went home praising God. Everyone was gripped with great wonder and awe. And they praised God, saying over and over again, "We have seen amazing things today."

Luke 5:17–26

Jesus traveled through all the cities and villages of that area, teaching in the synagogues and announcing the Good News about the Kingdom. And wherever he went, he healed people of every sort of disease and illness.

Matthew 9:35

A vast crowd brought him the lame, blind, crippled, mute, and many others with physical difficulties, and they laid them before Jesus. And he healed them all.

Matthew 15:30

. . .

[The Bible] has learned to speak in hundreds of languages to the heart of man.

Henry Van Dyke

. . .

Awe gripped the people as they saw this display of God's power. While everyone was marveling over all the wonderful things he was doing, Jesus said to his disciples, "Listen to me, and remember what I say. The Son of Man is going to be betrayed." But they didn't know what he meant. Its significance was hidden from them, so they could not understand it, and they were afraid to ask him about it.

Luke 9:43–45

JESUS CHRIST:
HIS MINISTRY

The Kingdom of Heaven

The disciples came to Jesus and asked, "Which of us is greatest in the Kingdom of Heaven?"

Jesus called a small child over to him and put the child among them. Then he said, "I assure you, unless you turn from your sins and become as little children, you will never get into the Kingdom of heaven. Therefore, anyone who becomes as humble as this little child is the greatest in the Kingdom of Heaven. And anyone who welcomes a little child like this on my behalf is welcoming me. But if anyone causes one of these little ones who trusts in me to lose faith, it would be better for that person to be thrown into the sea with a large millstone tied around the neck.

"Beware that you don't despise a single one of these little ones. For I tell you that in heaven their angels are always in the presence of my heavenly Father.

"In the same way, it is not my heavenly Father's will that even one of these little ones should perish."

But Jesus said, "Let the children come to me. Don't stop them! For the Kingdom of Heaven belongs to such as these."

Matthew 18:1–6, 10, 14; 19:14

In all my perplexities and distresses,
the Bible has never failed to
give me light and strength.

—Robert E. Lee

Jesus asked, "How can I describe the Kingdom of God? What story should I use to illustrate it?"

Mark 4:30

. . .

To my mind the most poignant mystical
exhortation ever written is
"be still and know that I am God."
—Arnold Bennett

. . .

"The Kingdom of Heaven is like a treasure that a man discovered hidden in a field. In his excitement, he hid it again and sold everything he owned to get enough money to buy the field—and to get the treasure, too!

"Again, the Kingdom of Heaven is like a pearl merchant on the look-out for choice pearls. When he discovered a pearl of great value, he sold everything he owned and bought it!

"Again, the Kingdom of Heaven is like a fishing net that is thrown into the water and gathers fish of very kind. When the net is full, they drag it up onto the shore, sit down, sort the good fish into crates, and throw the bad ones away. That is the way it will be at the end of the world. The angels will come and separate the wicked people from the godly, throwing the wicked into the fire. There will be weeping and gnashing of teeth."

Matthew 13:44–50

"However, no one knows the day or hour when these things will happen, not even the angels in heaven or the son himself. Only the Father knows. And since you don't know when they will happen, stay alert and keep watch."

Mark 13:32–33

Here is another illustration Jesus used: "The Kingdom of Heaven is like a mustard seed planted in a field. It is the smallest of all seeds, but it becomes the largest of garden plants and grows into a tree where birds can come and find shelter in its branches."

Matthew 13:31–32

Jesus Sends Out His Disciples

One day soon afterward Jesus went to a mountain to pray, and he prayed to God all night.

Luke 6:12

The Lord now chose seventy-two other disciples and sent them on ahead in pairs to all the towns and villages he planned to visit. These were his instructions to them: "The harvest is so great, but the workers are so few. Pray to the Lord who is in charge of the harvest, and ask him to send out more workers for his fields. Go now, and remember that I am sending you out as lambs among wolves. Don't take along any money, or a traveler's bag, or even an extra pair of sandals. And don't stop to greet anyone on the road.

"Whenever you enter a home, give it your blessing. If those who live there are worthy, the blessing will stand; if they are not, the blessing will return to you. As you heal them, say, 'The Kingdom of God is near you now.' Anyone who accepts your message is also accepting me. And anyone who rejects you is rejecting me. And anyone who rejects me is rejecting God who sent me."

Luke 10:1–6, 9, 16

When Jesus had finished saying all these things, he looked up to heaven and said, "Father, the time has come. Glorify your Son so he can give glory back to you. For you have given him authority over everyone in all the earth. He gives eternal life to each one you have given him.

"I have told these men about you. They were in the world, but then you gave them to me. Actually, they were always yours, and you gave them to me; and they have kept your word. For I have passed on to them the words you gave me; and they accepted them and know that I came from you, and they believe you sent me.

"My prayer is not for the world, but for those you have given me, because they belong to you. Now I am departing the world; I am leaving them behind and coming to you. Holy Father, keep them and care for them—all those you have given me—so that they will be united just as we are. During my time here, I have kept them safe. I guarded them so that not one was lost, except the one headed for destruction, as the Scriptures foretold.

"And now I am coming to you. I have told them many things while I was with them so they would be filled with my joy. I have given them your word. And the world hates them because they do not belong to the world, just as I do not. I'm not asking you to take them out of the world, but to keep them safe from the evil one. Make them pure and holy by teaching them your words of truth. As you sent me into the world, I am sending them into the world.

"I am praying not only for these disciples but also for all who will ever believe in me because of their testimony.

"I have given them the glory you gave me, so that they may be one, as we are.

"O, righteous Father, the world doesn't know you, but I do; and these disciples know you sent me. And I have revealed you to them and will keep on revealing you. I will do this so that your love for me may be in them and I in them."

John 17:1–2, 6, 8–9, 11–15, 17–18, 20, 22, 25–26

. . .

Only this I know, that one celestial Father gives to all.

John Milton

. . .

"I brought glory to you here on earth by doing everything you told me to do. And now, Father, bring me into the glory we shared before the world began."

JESUS CHRIST:
HIS MINISTRY

One controlling, guiding,
unifying mind must have been
operative through all the weary ages
to produce out of such composite elements
a result so wonderfully unique,
uplifting, and unfathomable as the Bible;
and that mind in the nature of things
could not have been human.

—William Gladstone

When the seventy-two disciples returned, they joyfully reported to him, "Lord, even the demons obey us when we use your name!"

"And I have given you authority over all the power of the enemy, and you can walk among snakes and scorpions and crush them. Nothing will injure you. But don't rejoice just because evil spirits obey you; rejoice because your names are registered as citizens of heaven."

Luke 10:17, 19–20

"But now I am going away to the one who sent me, and none of you has asked me where I am going. But it is actually best for you that I go away, because if I don't, the Counselor won't come. If I do go away, he will come because I will send him to you. And when he comes, he will convince the world of its sin, and of God's righteousness, and of the coming judgment. The world's sin is unbelief in me. Righteousness is available because I go to the Father, and you will see me no more. Judgment will come because the prince of this world has already been judged.

"When the Spirit of truth comes, he will guide you into all truth. He will not be presenting his own ideas; he will be telling you what he has heard. He will tell you about the future. He will bring me glory by revealing to you whatever he receives from me. All that the Father has is mine; this is what I mean when I say that the Spirit will reveal to you whatever he receives from me.

"In just a little while I will be gone, and you won't see me anymore. Then, just a little while after that, you will see me again."

John 16:5, 7–11, 13–16

JESUS CHRIST:
HIS MINISTRY

"Don't be troubled. You trust God, now trust me. There are many rooms in my Father's home, and I am going to prepare a place for you. If this were not so, I would tell you plainly. When everything is ready, I will come and get you, so that you will always be with me where I am."

John 14:1–3

"But the time is coming—in fact, it is already here—when you will be scattered, each one going his own way, leaving me alone. Yet I am not alone because the Father is with me. I have told you all this so that you may have peace in me. Here on earth you will have many trials and sorrows. But take heart, because I have overcome the world."

John 16:32–33

. . .

God's promises are sealed to us but not dated.

Susanna Wesley

. . .

"At that time you won't need to ask me for anything. The truth is, you can go directly to the Father and ask him, and he will grant your request because you use my name. You haven't done this before. Ask, using my name, and you will receive, and you will have abundant joy. Then you will ask in my name."

John 16:23–24, 26

"But the time is soon coming when I, the Son of Man, will be sitting at God's right hand in the place of power."

They all shouted, "Then you claim you are the Son of God?"

And he replied, "You are right in saying that I am."

Luke 22:69–70

"You say that I am a king, and you are right.... I was born for that purpose. And I came to bring truth to the world. All who love the truth recognize that what I say is true."

John 18:37

When the Lord Jesus had finished talking with them, he was taken up into heaven and sat down in the place of honor at God's right hand. And the disciples went everywhere and preached, and the Lord worked with them, confirming what they said by many miraculous signs.

Mark 16:19–20

Jesus' disciples saw him do many other miraculous signs besides the ones recorded in this book. But these are written so that you may believe that Jesus is the Messiah, the Son of God, and that by believing in him you will have life.

John 20:30–31

The Name of Jesus

History, without God,
is a chaos without design, or end, or aim.
Political economy without God would be a
selfish teaching about the acquisition of wealth.
Physics without God would be but a dull enquiry
into certain meaningless phenomena.
All sciences may do good service, if those who
cultivate them know their place.

—Edward B. Pusey

For there is only one God and one Mediator who can reconcile God and people. He is the man Christ Jesus. He gave his life to purchase freedom for everyone. This is the message that God gave to the world at the proper time.

I Timothy 2:5–6

This shows that God's Son is far greater than the angels, just as the name God gave him is far greater than their names.

Hebrews 1:4

You gave him authority over all things. Now when it says "all things, " it means nothing is left out. But we have not yet seen all of this happen.

Hebrews 2:8

And in human form he obediently humbled himself even further by dying a criminal's death on a cross. Because of this, God raised him up to the heights of heaven and gave him a name that is above every other name, so that at the name of Jesus every knee will bow, in heaven and on earth and under the earth, and every tongue will confess that Jesus Christ is Lord, to the glory of God the Father.

Philippians 2:8–11

But although the world was made through him, the world didn't recognize him when he came. But to all who believed him and accepted him, he gave the right to become children of God.

John 1:10, 12

"I have been given complete authority in heaven and on earth. You can ask for anything in my name, and I will do it, because the work of the Son brings glory to the Father. Yes, ask anything in my name, and I will do it!"

Matthew 28:18; John 14:13–14

. . .

I know the Bible is inspired because
it finds me at a greater depth of
my being than any other book.

Samuel Taylor Coleridge

. . .

"The truth is, you can go directly to the Father and ask him, and he will grant your request because you use my name. And I will give you the keys of the Kingdom of Heaven. Whatever you lock on earth will be locked in heaven, and whatever you open on earth will be opened in heaven."

John 16:23; Matthew 16:19

"These signs will accompany those who believe: They will cast out demons in my name, and they will speak new languages. They will be able to handle snakes with safety, and if they drink anything poisonous, it won't hurt them. They will be able to place their hands on the sick and heal them."

Mark 16:17–18

HOLY GHOST, SPIRIT, SPIRIT OF GOD, COMFORTER, SPIRIT OF TRUTH

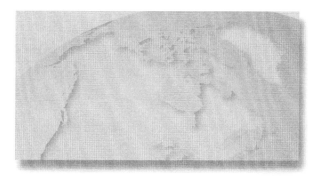

To believe in God is to know
that all the rules will be fair—
and that there will be
wonderful surprises!

—Mary Corita

The earth was empty, a formless mass cloaked in darkness. And the Spirit of God was hovering over its surface. Then God said, "Let there be light," and there was light.

Genesis 1:2–3

One day when the crowds were being baptized, Jesus himself was baptized. As he was praying, the heavens opened, and the Holy Spirit descended on him in the form of a dove. And a voice from heaven said, "You are my beloved Son, and I am fully pleased with you."

Luke 3:21–22

"In just a little while I will be gone, and you won't see me anymore."

John 16:16

"And I will ask the Father, and he will give you another Counselor, who will never leave you. He is the Holy Spirit, who leads into all truth. The world at large cannot receive him, because it isn't looking for him and doesn't recognize him. But you do, because he lives with you now and later will be in you. No, I will not abandon you as orphans—I will come to you."

John 14:16–18

"But it is actually best for you that I go away, because if I don't, the Counselor won't come. If I do go away, he will come because I will send him to you. And when he comes, he will convince the world of its sin, and of God's righteousness, and of the coming judgment."

John 16:7–8

"But when the Father sends the Counselor as my representative—and by the Counselor I mean the Holy Spirit—he will teach you everything and will remind you of everything I myself have told you."

John 14:26

. . .

When you have nothing left but God,
then you become aware that God is enough.

Agnes Royden

. . .

"When the Spirit of truth comes, he will guide you into all truth. He will not be presenting his own ideas; he will be telling you what he has heard. He will tell you about the future. He will bring me glory by revealing to you whatever he receives from me."

John 16:13–14

"But I will send you the Counselor—the Spirit of truth. He will come to you from the Father and will tell you all about me."

John 15:26

So I want you to know how to discern what is truly from God: No one speaking by the Spirit of God can curse Jesus, and no one is able to say, "Jesus is Lord," except by the Holy Spirit.

I Corinthians 12:3

This is the way to find out if they have the Spirit of God: If a prophet acknowledges that Jesus Christ became a human being, that person has the Spirit of God. If a prophet does not acknowledge Jesus, that person is not from God. Such a person has the spirit of the Antichrist. You have heard that he is going to come into the world, and he is already here.

But we belong to God; that is why those who know God listen to us. If they do not belong to God, they do not listen to us. That is how we know if someone has the Spirit of truth or the spirit of deception.

I John 4:2–3, 6

But you are not controlled by your sinful nature. You are controlled by the Spirit if you have the Spirit of God living in you. (And remember that those who do not have the Spirit of Christ living in them are not Christians at all.) Since Christ lives within you, even though your body will die because of sin, your spirit is alive because you have been made right with God.

If through the power of the Holy Spirit you turn from it and its evil deeds, you will live. For all who are led by the Spirit of God are children of God.

Romans 8:9–10, 13–14

But people who aren't Christians can't understand these truths from God's Spirit. It all sounds foolish to them because only those who have the Spirit can understand what the Spirit means.

I Corinthians 2:14

And now, why delay? Get up and be baptized, and have your sins washed away, calling on the name of the Lord.

Each of you must turn from your sins and turn to God, and be baptized in the name of Jesus Christ for the forgiveness of your sins. Then you will receive the gift of the Holy Spirit.

Acts 22:16; 2:38

. . .

He has sounded forth the trumpet
that shall never call retreat ;
He is sifting out the hearts of men
before his judgment seat.

Julia Ward Howe

. . .

"I assure you that any sin can be forgiven, including blasphemy, but anyone who blasphemes against the Holy Spirit will never be forgiven. It is an eternal sin."

Mark 3:28–29

And the Holy Spirit helps us in our distress. For we don't even know what we should pray for, nor how we should pray. But the Holy Spirit prays for us with groanings that cannot be expressed in words. And the Father who knows all hearts knows what the Spirit is saying, for the Spirit pleads for us believers in harmony with God's own will.

Romans 8:26–27

As long as I live, while I have breath from God, my lips will speak no evil, and my tongue will speak no lies.

I speak with all sincerity; I speak the truth. For the Spirit of God has made me, and the breath of the Almighty gives me life.

Job 27:3–4; 33:3–4

And Jesus Christ was revealed as God's Son by his baptism in water and by shedding his blood on the cross—not by water only, but by water and blood. And the Spirit also gives us the testimony that this is true. So we have these three witnesses—the Spirit, the water, and the blood— and all three agree.

1 John 5:6–7

And do not bring sorrow to God's Holy Spirit by the way you live. Remember, he is the one who has identified you as his own, guaranteeing that you will be saved on the day of redemption.

Get rid of all bitterness, rage, anger, harsh words, and slander, as well as all types of malicious behavior.

Ephesians 4:30–31

"Every sin or blasphemy can be forgiven—except blasphemy against the Holy Spirit, which can never be forgiven. Anyone who blasphemes against me, the Son of Man, can be forgiven, but blasphemy against the Holy Spirit will never be forgiven, either in this world or in the world to come."

Matthew 12:31–32

. . .

A man can no more diminish God's glory by refusing to worship him than a lunatic can put out the sun by scribbling the word "darkness" on the walls of his cell.

C. S. Lewis

. . .

"And so I tell you, keep on asking, and you will be given what you ask for. Keep on looking, and you will find. Keep on knocking, and the door will be opened. You fathers—if your children ask for a fish, do you give them a snake instead? Or if they ask for an egg, do you give them a scorpion? Of course not! If you sinful people know how to give good gifts to your children, how much more will your heavenly Father give the Holy Spirit to those who ask him."

Luke 11:9, 11–13

The Armor of God

*God reveals himself
unfailingly to
the thoughtful seeker.*

—Honoré de Balzac

A final word: Be strong with the Lord's mighty power. Put on all of God's armor so that you will be able to stand firm against all strategies and tricks of the Devil. For we are not fighting against people made of flesh and blood, but against the evil rulers and authorities of the unseen world, against those mighty powers of darkness who rule this world, and against wicked spirits in the heavenly realms.

Use every piece of God's armor to resist the enemy in the time of evil, so that after the battle you will still be standing firm. Stand your ground, putting on the sturdy belt of truth and the body armor of God's righteousness. For shoes, put on the peace that comes from the Good News, so that you will be fully prepared. In every battle you will need faith as your shield to stop the fiery arrows aimed at you by Satan. Put on salvation as your helmet, and take the sword of the Spirit, which is the word of God. Pray at all times and on every occasion in the power of the Holy Spirit. Stay alert and be persistent in your prayers for all Christians everywhere.

Ephesians 6:10–18

. . .

God is the light in my darkness,
the voice in my silence.

Helen Keller

. . .

But in that coming day, no weapon turned against you will succeed. And everyone who tells lies in court will be brought to justice. These benefits are enjoyed by the servants of the LORD; their vindication will come from me. I, the LORD, have spoken!

Isaiah 54:17

Fight the good fight for what we believe. Hold tightly to the eternal life that God has given you, which you have confessed so well before many witnesses.

1 Timothy 6:12

And I am convinced that nothing can ever separate us from his love. Death can't, and life can't. The angels can't, and demons can't. Our fears for today, our worries about tomorrow, and even the powers of hell can't keep God's love away. Whether we are high above the sky or in the deepest ocean, nothing in all creation will ever be able to separate us from the love of God that is revealed in Christ Jesus our Lord.

Romans 8:38–39

Christ is the one through whom God created everything in heaven and earth. He made the things we can see and the things we can't see— kings, kingdoms, rulers, and authorities. Everything has been created through him and for him. He existed before everything else began, and he holds all creation together.

Colossians 1:16–17

What can we say about such wonderful things as these? If God is for us, who can ever be against us? Since God did not spare even his own Son but gave him up for us all, won't God, who gave us Christ, also give us everything else?

Who dares accuse us whom God has chosen for his own? Will God? No! He is the one who has given us right standing with himself. Who then will condemn us? Will Christ Jesus? No, for he is the one who died for us and was raised to life for us and is sitting at the place of highest honor next to God, pleading for us.

Can anything ever separate us from Christ's love? Does it mean he no longer loves us if we have trouble or calamity, or are persecuted, or are hungry or cold or in danger or threatened with death? No, despite all these things, overwhelming victory is ours through Christ, who loved us.

For nothing is impossible with God.

Romans 8:31, 33–35, 37; Luke 1:37

. . .

The Bible is
a window in this prison-world
through which we may look into eternity.

Timothy Dwight

. . .

The Church

BODY OF CHRIST

Who knows?
God knows and what he knows
Is well and best.
The darkness hideth not from him,
but glows
Clear as the morning or the evening rose
Of east or west.

—Christina Rossetti

"I will build my church, and all the powers of hell will not conquer it. And I will give you the keys of the Kingdom of Heaven. Whatever you lock on earth will be locked in heaven, and whatever you open on earth will be opened in heaven."

Matthew 16:18–19

This is a great mystery, but it is an illustration of the way Christ and the church are one. You are reasonable people. Decide for yourselves if what I am about to say is true. And we all eat from one loaf, showing that we are one body.

Ephesians 5:32; I Corinthians 10:15, 17

. . .

A church is a hospital for sinners,
not a museum for saints.

L. L. Nash

. . .

Now all of you together are Christ's body, and each one of you is a separate and necessary part of it. Here is a list of some of the members that God has placed in the body of Christ: first are apostles, second are prophets, third are teachers, then those who do miracles, those who have the gift of healing, those who can help others, those who can get others to work together, those who speak in unknown languages.

I Corinthians 12:27–28

Their responsibility is to equip God's people to do his work and build up the church, the body of Christ, until we come to such unity in our faith and knowledge of God's Son that we will be mature and full grown in the Lord, measuring up to the full stature of Christ. We have all benefited from the rich blessings he brought to us—one gracious blessing after another.

Ephesians 4:12–13; John 1:16

For a husband is the head of his wife as Christ is the head of his body, the church; he gave his life to be her Savior. As the church submits to Christ, so you wives must submit to your husbands in everything.

And you husbands must love your wives with the same love Christ showed the church. He gave up his life for her. He did this to present her to himself as a glorious church without a spot or wrinkle or any other blemish. Instead, she will be holy and without fault. And we are his body.

Ephesians 5:23–25, 27, 30

What this means is that those who become Christians become new persons. They are not the same anymore, for the old life is gone. A new life has begun!

2 Corinthians 5:17

This is real love. It is not that we loved God, but that he loved us and sent his Son as a sacrifice to take away our sins. We love each other as a result of his loving us first.

1 John 4:10, 19

Now there are different kinds of spiritual gifts, but it is the same Holy Spirit who is the source of them all. There are different kinds of service in the church, but it is the same Lord we are serving. There are different ways God works in our lives, but it is the same God who does the work through all of us. A spiritual gift is given to each of us as a means of helping the entire church.

To one person the Spirit gives the ability to give wise advice; to another he gives the gift of special knowledge. The Spirit gives special faith to another, and to someone else he gives the power to heal the sick. He gives one person the power to perform miracles, and to another the ability to prophesy. He gives someone else the ability to know whether it is really the Spirit of God or another spirit that is speaking. Still another person is given the ability to speak in unknown languages, and another is given the ability to interpret what is being said. It is the one and only Holy Spirit who distributes these gifts. He alone decides which gift each person should have.

The human body has many parts, but the many parts make up only one body. So it is with the body of Christ. Some of us are Jews, some are Gentiles, some are slaves, and some are free. But we have all been baptized into Christ's body by one Spirit, and we have all received the same Spirit.

Yes, the body has many different parts, not just one part.

I Corinthians 12:4–14

We are all one body, we have the same Spirit, and we have all been called to the same glorious future. There is only one Lord, one faith, one baptism, and there is only one God and Father, who is over us all and in us all and living through us all. However, he has given each one of us a special gift according to the generosity of Christ.

Ephesians 4:4–7

And all who have been united with Christ in baptism have been made like him. There is no longer Jew or Gentile, slave or free, male or female. For you are all Christians—you are one in Christ Jesus. And now that you belong to Christ, you are the true children of Abraham. You are his heirs, and now all the promises God gave to him belong to you.

Galatians 3:27–29

So humble yourselves under the mighty power of God, and in his good time he will honor you. Give all your worries and cares to God, for he cares about what happens to you.

Be careful! Watch out for attacks from the Devil, your great enemy. He prowls around like a roaring lion, looking for some victim to devour. Take a firm stand against him, and be strong in your faith. Remember that Christians all over the world are going through the same kind of suffering you are.

I Peter 5:6–9

So you should not be like cowering, fearful slaves. You should behave instead like God's very own children, adopted into his family—calling him "Father, dear Father." For his Holy Spirit speaks to us deep in our hearts and tells us that we are God's children. And since we are his children, we will share his treasures—for everything God gives to his Son, Christ, is ours, too. But if we are to share his glory, we must also share his suffering.

Romans 8:15–17

Then we will no longer be like children, forever changing our minds about what we believe because someone has told us something different or because someone has cleverly lied to us and made the lie sound like the truth. Instead, we will hold to the truth in love, becoming more and more in every way like Christ, who is the head of his body, the church. So get rid of all the filth and evil in your lives, and humbly accept the message God has planted in your hearts, for it is strong enough to save your souls. And remember, it is a message to obey, not just to listen to. If you don't obey, you are only fooling yourself. And whatever you do or say, let it be as a representative of the Lord Jesus, all the while giving thanks through him to God the Father.

Ephesians 4:14–15; James 1; 21–22; Colossians 3:17

Study this Book of the Law continually. Meditate on it day and night so you may be sure to obey all that is written in it. Only then will you succeed.

Joshua 1:8

If the person who doesn't attend church because hypocrites do were consistent, he wouldn't attend anything.

—Olin Miller

All Scripture is inspired by God and is useful to teach us what is true and to make us realize what is wrong in our lives. It straightens us out and teaches us to do what is right. It is God's way of preparing us in every way, fully equipped for every good thing God wants us to do.

2 Timothy 3:16–17

. . .

It is not with the motes from one's neighbor's eye
that the house of God can be built,
but with the beam that one takes out of one's own.

André Gide

. . .

So do not be attracted by strange, new ideas. Your spiritual strength comes from God's special favor. Don't forget to do good and to share what you have with those in need, for such sacrifices are very pleasing to God.

Hebrews 13:9, 16

Christ is the head of the church, which is his body. He is the first of all who will rise from the dead, so he is first in everything. For God in all his fullness was pleased to live in Christ.

Colossians 1:18, 19

So don't get tired of doing what is good. Don't get discouraged and give up, for we will reap a harvest of blessing at the appropriate time. Whenever we have the opportunity, we should do good to everyone, especially to our Christian brothers and sisters. Remember that the Lord will reward each one of us for the good we do, whether we are slaves or free.

Galatians 6:9–10; Ephesians 6:8

Anyone who is willing to hear should listen to the Spirit and understand what the Spirit is saying to the churches. Everyone who is victorious will eat from the tree of life in the paradise of God. Yet even in Sardis there are some who have not soiled their garments with evil deeds. They will walk with me in white, for they are worthy. All who are victorious will be clothed in white. I will never erase their names from the Book of Life, but I will announce before my Father and his angels that they are mine. Anyone who is willing to hear should listen to the Spirit and understand what the Spirit is saying to the churches.

Revelation 2:7; 3:4–6

"Go into all the world and preach the Good News to everyone, everywhere. Anyone who believes and is baptized will be saved. But anyone who refuses to believe will be condemned."

Mark 16:15–16

Be strong and courageous! Do not be afraid or discouraged. For the LORD your God is with you wherever you go.

Joshua 1:9

He paints the lily of the field,
  Perfumes each lily bell;
If he so loves the little flowers,
  I know he loves me well.

—Maria Straus

Spirit
v.
Flesh

*The Bible was never intended to be
a book for scholars and specialists only.
From the very beginning
it was intended to be everybody's book,
and that is what it continues to be.*

—F. F. Bruce

"You can enter God's Kingdom only through the narrow gate. The high-way to hell is broad, and its gate is wide for the many who choose the easy way. But the gateway to life is small, and the road is narrow, and only a few ever find it."

Matthew 7:13–14

"The door to heaven is narrow. Work hard to get in, because many will try to enter."

Luke 13:24

Don't be misled. Remember that you can't ignore God and get away with it. You will always reap what you sow! Those who live only to satisfy their own sinful desires will harvest the consequences of decay and death. But those who live to please the Spirit will harvest everlasting life from the Spirit.

Galatians 6:7–8

So I advise you to live according to your new life in the Holy Spirit. Then you won't be doing what your sinful nature craves. The old sinful nature loves to do evil, which is just opposite from what the Holy Spirit wants. And the Spirit gives us desires that are opposite from what the sinful nature desires. These two forces are constantly fighting each other, and your choices are never free from this conflict.

Galatians 5:16–17

When you follow the desires of your sinful nature, your lives will produce these evil results: sexual immorality, impure thoughts, eagerness for lustful pleasure, idolatry, participation in demonic activities, hostility, quarreling, jealousy, outbursts of anger, selfish ambition, divisions, the feeling that everyone is wrong except those in your own little group, envy, drunkenness, wild parties, and other kinds of sin. Let me tell you again as I have before, that anyone living that sort of life will not inherit the Kingdom of God.

But when the Holy Spirit controls our lives, he will produce this kind of fruit in us: love, joy, peace, patience, kindness, goodness, faithfulness, gentleness, and self-control. Here there is no conflict with the law.

Those who belong to Christ Jesus have nailed the passions and desires of their sinful nature to his cross and crucified them there. If we are living now by the Holy Spirit, let us follow the Holy Spirit's leading in every part of our lives. Let us not become conceited, or irritate one another, or be jealous of one another.

Galatians 5:19–26

"For God is Spirit, so those who worship him must worship in spirit and in truth."

John 4 :24

"It is the Spirit who gives eternal life. Human effort accomplishes nothing. And the very words I have spoken to you are spirit and life."

John 6:63

Those who are dominated by the sinful nature think about sinful things, but those who are controlled by the Holy Spirit think about things that please the Spirit. If your sinful nature controls your mind, there is death. But if the Holy Spirit controls your mind, there is life and peace. For the sinful nature is always hostile to God. It never did obey God's laws, and it never will. That's why those who are still under the control of their sinful nature can never please God.

But you are not controlled by your sinful nature. You are controlled by the Spirit if you have the Spirit of God living in you. (And remember that those who do not have the Spirit of Christ living in them are not Christians at all.)

Romans 8:5–9

. . .

Give the Bible to the people, unadulterated,
pure, unaltered, unexplained, uncheapened,
and then see it work through the whole nature.

Woodrow Wilson

. . .

He personally carried away our sins in his own body on the cross so we can be dead to sin and live for what is right. You have been healed by his wounds! Once you were wandering like lost sheep. But now you have turned to your Shepherd, the Guardian of your souls.

I Peter 2:24–25

But God is so rich in mercy, and he loved us so very much, that even while we were dead because of our sins, he gave us life when he raised Christ from the dead. (It is only by God's special favor that you have been saved!) For he raised us from the dead along with Christ, and we are seated with him in the heavenly realms—all because we are one with Christ Jesus. And so God can always point to us as examples of the incredible wealth of his favor and kindness toward us, as shown in all he has done for us through Christ Jesus.

Ephesians 2:4–7

His unchanging plan has always been to adopt us into his own family by bringing us to himself through Jesus Christ. And this gave him great pleasure.

So we praise God for the wonderful kindness he has poured out on us because we belong to his dearly loved Son. He is so rich in kindness that he purchased our freedom through the blood of his Son, and our sins are forgiven. He has showered his kindness on us, along with all wisdom and understanding.

God's secret plan has now been revealed to us; it is a plan centered on Christ, designed long ago according to his good pleasure.

Ephesians 1:5–9

For no one can ever be made right in God's sight by doing what his law commands. For the more we know God's law, the clearer it becomes that we aren't obeying it. So we are made right with God through faith and not by obeying the law.

Romans 3:20, 28

It was said, sneeringly, by someone that
if a clam could conceive of God,
it would conceive of him in the shape of
a great, big clam. Naturally.
And if God has revealed himself to clams,
it could only be under
conditions of perfect clamhood,
since any other manifestation would be
wholly irrelevant to clam nature.

—Dorothy L. Sayers

Don't forget that you Gentiles used to be outsiders by birth. You were called "the uncircumcised ones" by the Jews, who were proud of their circumcision, even though it affected only their bodies and not their hearts. In those days you were living apart from Christ. You were excluded from God's people, Israel, and you did not know the promises God had made to them. You lived in this world without God and without hope. But now you belong to Christ Jesus. Though you once were far away from God, now you have been brought near to him because of the blood of Christ.

For Christ himself has made peace between us Jews and you Gentiles by making us all one people. He has broken down the wall of hostility that used to separate us. By his death he ended the whole system of Jewish law that excluded the Gentiles. His purpose was to make peace between Jews and Gentiles by creating in himself one new person from the two groups. Together as one body, Christ reconciled both groups to God by means of his death, and our hostility toward each other was put to death.

Ephesians 2:11–16

So now there is no condemnation for those who belong to Christ Jesus. For the power of the life-giving Spirit has freed you through Christ Jesus from the power of sin that leads to death. The law of Moses could not save us, because of our sinful nature. But God put into effect a different plan to save us. He sent his own Son in a human body like ours, except that ours are sinful. God destroyed sin's control over us by giving his Son as a sacrifice for our sins. He did this so that the requirement of the law would be fully accomplished for us who no longer follow our sinful nature but instead follow the Spirit.

Romans 8:1–4

But you are not controlled by your sinful nature. You are controlled by the Spirit if you have the Spirit of God living in you. (And remember that those who do not have the Spirit of Christ living in them are not Christians at all.) Since Christ lives within you, even though your body will die because of sin, your spirit is alive because you have been made right with God. The Spirit of God, who raised Jesus from the dead, lives in you. And just as he raised Christ from the dead, he will give life to your mortal body by this same Spirit living within you.

So dear Christian friends, you have no obligation whatsoever to do what your sinful nature urges you to do. For if you keep on following it, you will perish. But if through the power of the Holy Spirit you turn from it and its evil deeds, you will live. For all who are led by the Spirit of God are children of God.

Romans 8:9–14

Well then, should we keep on sinning so that God can show us more and more kindness and forgiveness? Of course not! Since we have died to sin, how can we continue to live in it? Or have you forgotten that when we became Christians and were baptized to become one with Christ Jesus, we died with him? For we died and were buried with Christ by baptism. And just as Christ was raised from the dead by the glorious power of the Father, now we also may live new lives.

Since we have been united with him in his death, we will also be raised as he was. Our old sinful selves were crucified with Christ so that sin might lose its power in our lives. We are no longer slaves to sin.

Romans 6:1–6

This is real love. It is not that we loved God, but that he loved us and sent his Son as a sacrifice to take away ours sins.

Dear friends, since God loved us that much, we surely ought to love each other. No one has ever seen God. But if we love each other, God lives in us, and his love has been brought to full expression through us.

And God has given us his Spirit as proof that we live in him, and he in us. Furthermore, we have seen with our own eyes and now testify that the Father sent his Son to be the Savior of the world.

I John 4:10–14

. . .

The perfection of human expression was achieved
when the world was younger:
The Song of Songs, which is Solomon's,
the Book of Psalms,
the Revelation of John the Divine.

Fannie Hurst

. . .

We are sure of this because Christ rose from the dead, and he will never die again. Death no longer has any power over him. He died once to defeat sin, and now he lives for the glory of God. So you should consider yourselves dead to sin and able to live for the glory of God through Christ Jesus.

Romans 6:9–11

But people who aren't Christians can't understand these truths from God's Spirit. It all sounds foolish to them because only those who have the Spirit can understand what the Spirit means.

1 Corinthians 2:14

When I think of the wisdom and scope of God's plan, I fall to my knees and pray to the Father, the Creator of everything in heaven and on earth. I pray that from his glorious, unlimited resources he will give you mighty inner strength through his Holy Spirit. And I pray that Christ will be more and more at home in your hearts as you trust in him. May your roots go down deep into the soil of God's marvelous love. And may you have the power to understand, as all God's people should, how wide, how long, how high, and how deep his love really is. May you experience the love of Christ, though it is so great you will never fully understand it. Then you will be filled with the fullness of life and power that comes from God.

Ephesians 3:14–19

All honor to the God and Father of our Lord Jesus Christ, for it is by his boundless mercy that God has given us the privilege of being born again. Now we live with a wonderful expectation because Jesus Christ rose again from the dead. For God has reserved a priceless inheritance for his children. It is kept in heaven for you, pure and undefiled, beyond the reach of change and decay. And God, in his mighty power, will protect you until you receive this salvation, because you are trusting him. It will be revealed on the last day for all to see.

1 Peter 1:3–5

He wrote no book,
and yet his words and prayer
Are intimate on many myriad tongues,
Are counsel everywhere.

—Therese Lindsey

A man can accept what
Christ has done without knowing
how it works;
indeed, he certainly won't know
how it works until he's accepted it.

—C. S. Lewis

"Have faith in God. I assure you that you can say to this mountain, 'May God lift you up and throw you into the sea,' and your command will be obeyed. All that's required is that you really believe and do not doubt in your heart. What you have believed has happened."

Mark 11:22–23; Matthew 8:13

"Anything is possible if a person believes. Humanly speaking, it is impossible. But not with God. Everything is possible with God."

Mark 9:23; 10:27

"Because of your faith, it will happen."

Matthew 9:29

What is faith? It is the confident assurance that what we hope for is going to happen. It is the evidence of things we cannot yet see. By faith we understand that the entire universe was formed at God's command, that what we now see did not come from anything that can be seen.

Hebrews 11:1, 3

It was by faith that Abraham offered Isaac, as a sacrifice when God was testing him. Abraham, who had received God's promises, was ready to sacrifice his only son, Isaac. Abraham assumed that if Isaac died, God was able to bring him back to life again. And in a sense, Abraham did receive his son back from the dead.

Hebrews 11:17, 19

It was by faith that Noah built an ark to save his family from the flood. He obeyed God, who warned him about something that had never happened before. By his faith he condemned the rest of the world and was made right in God's sight.

It was by faith that Abraham obeyed when God called him to leave home and go to another land that God would give him as his inheritance. He went without knowing where he was going.

Hebrews 11:7–8

. . .

*Faith is an affirmation and an act
that bids eternal truth be fact.*

George Pope Morris

. . .

When God promised Abraham that he would become the father of many nations, Abraham believed him. God had also said, "Your descendants will be as numerous as the stars," even though such a promise seemed utterly impossible! And Abraham's faith did not weaken, even though he knew that he was too old to be a father at the age of one hundred and that Sarah, his wife, had never been able to have children. Abraham never wavered in believing God's promise. In fact, his faith grew stronger, and in this he brought glory to God.

Romans 4:18–20

He was absolutely convinced that God was able to do anything he promised. And because of Abraham's faith, God declared him to be righteous.

Romans 4:21–22

Dear brothers and sisters, what's the use of saying you have faith if you don't prove it by your actions? That kind of faith can't save anyone.

So you see, it isn't enough just to have faith. Faith that doesn't show itself by good deeds is no faith at all—it is dead and useless.

Now someone may argue, "Some people have faith; others have good deeds." I say, "I can't see your faith if you don't have good deeds, but I will show you my faith through my good deeds."

Don't you remember that our ancestor Abraham was declared right with God because of what he did when he offered his son Isaac on the altar? You see, he was trusting God so much that he was willing to do whatever God told him to do. His faith was made complete by what he did—by his actions. So you see, we are made right with God by what we do, not by faith alone.

Just as the body is dead without a spirit, so also faith is dead without good deeds.

James 2:14, 17–18, 21–22, 24, 26

"You believe because you have seen me. Blessed are those who haven't seen me and believe anyway."

John 20:29

Well then, if we emphasize faith, does this mean that we can forget about the law? Of course not! In fact, only when we have faith do we truly fulfill the law.

Abraham was humanly speaking the founder of our Jewish nation. What were his experiences concerning this question of being saved by faith? Was it because of his good deeds that God accepted him? If so, he would have had something to boast about. But from God's point of view Abraham had no basis at all for pride. For the Scriptures tell us, "Abraham believed God, so God declared him to be righteous."

It is clear, then, that God's promise to give the whole earth to Abraham and his descendants was not based on obedience to God's law, but on the new relationship with God that comes by faith.

Romans 3:31–4:3, 13

God will surely do this for you, for he always does just what he says.

I Corinthians 1:9

It was by faith that Moses, when he grew up, refused to be treated as the son of Pharaoh's daughter. He chose to share the oppression of God's people instead of enjoying the fleeting pleasures of sin. He thought it was better to suffer for the sake of the Messiah than to own the treasures of Egypt, for he was looking ahead to the great reward that God would give him. It was by faith that Moses left the land of Egypt. He was not afraid of the king. Moses kept right on going because he kept his eyes on the one who is invisible.

Hebrews 11:24–27

These trials are only to test your faith, to show that it is strong and pure. It is being tested as fire tests and purifies gold—and your faith is far more precious to God than mere gold. So if your faith remains strong after being tried by fiery trials it will bring you much praise and glory and honor on the day when Jesus Christ is revealed to the whole world.

You love him even though you have never seen him. Though you do not see him, you trust him, and even now you are happy with a glorious, inexpressible joy. Your reward for trusting him will be the salvation of your souls.

I Peter 1:7–9

. . .

Faith is for that which lies on the other side of reason.
Faith is what makes life bearable,
with all its tragedies and ambiguities,
and sudden, startling joys.

Madeleine L'Engle

. . .

You may have the faith to believe that there is nothing wrong with what you are doing, but keep it between yourself and God. . . . If you do anything you believe is not right, you are sinning. Examine yourselves to see if your faith is really genuine. Test yourselves.

Romans 14:22–23; 2 Corinthians 13:5

Faith is not anti-intellectual.
It is an act of
man that reaches beyond
the limits of our five senses.

—Billy Graham

And my message and my preaching were very plain. I did not use wise and persuasive speeches, but the Holy Spirit was powerful among you. I did this so that you might trust the power of God rather than human wisdom.

1 Corinthians 2:4–5,

And let us run with endurance the race that God has set before us. We do this by keeping our eyes on Jesus, on who our faith depends from start to finish. So you are all children of God through faith in Christ Jesus. That is why we live by believing and not by seeing.

Hebrews 12:1–2; Galatians 3:26; 2 Corinthians 5:7

Therefore, since we have been made right in God's sight by faith, we have peace with God because of what Jesus Christ our Lord has done for us. Because of our faith, Christ has brought us into this place of highest privilege where we now stand, and we confidently and joyfully look forward to sharing God's glory.

We can rejoice, too, when we run into problems and trials, for we know that they are good for us—they help us learn to endure. And endurance develops strength of character in us, and character strengthens our confident expectation of salvation. And this expectation will not disappoint us. For we know how dearly God loves us, because he has given us the Holy Spirit to fill our hearts with his love.

Romans 5:1–5

So we don't look at the troubles we can see right now; rather, we look forward to what we have not yet seen. For the troubles we see will soon be over, but the joys to come will last forever.

2 Corinthians 4:18

So, you see, it is impossible to please God without faith. Anyone who wants to come to him must believe that there is a God and that he rewards those who sincerely seek him.

Hebrews 11:6

. . .

Faith is to believe what we do not see;
and the reward of this faith is
to see what we believe.

Augustine of Hippo

. . .

But how can they call on him to save them unless they believe in him? And how can they believe in him if they have never heard about him? And how can they hear about him unless someone tells them? Yet faith comes from listening to this message of good news—the Good News about Christ.

Romans 10:14, 17

"I am leaving you with a gift—peace of mind and heart. And the peace I give isn't like the peace the world gives. So don't be troubled or afraid."

John 14:27

For God is not a God of disorder but of peace, as in all the other churches. That is why we can say with confidence, "The Lord is my helper, so I will not be afraid. What can mere mortals do to me?"

1 Corinthians 14:33; Hebrews 13:6

The LORD is for me, so I will not be afraid. What can mere mortals do to me?
   It is better to trust the LORD than to put confidence in people.
   The LORD is my strength and my song: he has become my victory.
   I thank you for answering my prayer and saving me!"
   Yes, and the LORD will deliver me from every evil attack and will bring me safely to his heavenly Kingdom. To God be the glory forever and ever. Amen.

Psalm 118:6, 8, 14, 21; 2 Timothy 4:18

The LORD says, "I will rescue those who love me. I will protect those who trust in my name. When they call on me, I will answer; I will be with them in trouble. I will rescue them and honor them. I will satisfy them with a long life and give them my salvation."

Psalm 91:14–16

My experience is that
Christianity dispels more mystery
than it involves.
With Christianity it is
twilight in the world;
without it, night.

—Anne Sophie Swetchine

The Tongue

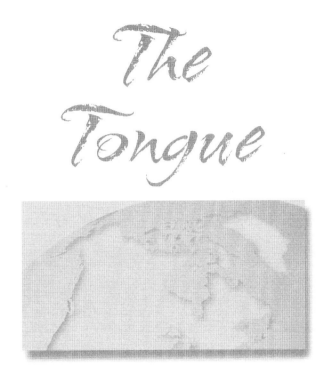

Whatever weakens your reason,
impairs the tenderness of your conscience,
obscures your sense of God,
and takes off the relish of spiritual things—
that to you is sin.

—Susanna Wesley

"I have sworn by my own name, and I will never go back on my word: Every knee will bow to me, and every tongue will confess allegiance to my name."

The people will declare, "The LORD is the source of all my righteousness and strength." And all who were angry with him will come to him and be ashamed.

Isaiah 45:23–24

And every tongue will confess that Jesus Christ is Lord, to the glory of God the Father.

Philippians 2:11

For the Scriptures say, "'As surely as I live,' says the Lord, 'every knee will bow to me and every tongue will confess allegiance to God.'" Yes, each of us will have to give a personal account to God. So don't condemn each other anymore. Decide instead to live in such a way that you will not put an obstacle in another Christian's path.

Romans 14:11–13

Above all else, guard your heart, for it affects everything you do. Avoid all perverse talk; stay far from corrupt speech.

Proverbs 4:23–24

Those who control their tongue will have a long life; a quick retort can ruin everything.

Proverbs 13:3

Words satisfy the soul as food satisfies the stomach; the right words on a person's lips bring satisfaction. Those who love to talk will experience the consequences, for the tongue can kill or nourish life.

Proverbs 18:20–21

Don't speak evil against each other, my dear brothers and sisters. If you criticize each other and condemn each other, then you are criticizing and condemning God's law. But you are not a judge who can decide whether the law is right or wrong. Your job is to obey it. Don't grumble about each other, my brothers and sisters, or God will judge you. For look! The great judge is coming. He is standing at the door! God alone, who made the law, can rightly judge among us. He alone has the power to save or to destroy. So what right do you have to condemn your neighbor?

James 4:11; 5:9; 4:12

"Listen to what I say and try to understand. You are not defiled by what you eat; you are defiled by what you say and do."

Matthew 15:10–11

So also, the tongue is a small thing, but what enormous damage it can do. A tiny spark can set a great forest on fire. And the tongue is a flame of fire. It is full of wickedness that can ruin your whole life. It can turn the entire course of your life into a blazing flame of destruction, for it is set on fire by hell itself.

James 3:5–6

"You brood of snakes! How could evil men like you speak what is good and right? For whatever is in your heart determines what you say. A good person produces good words from a good heart, and an evil person produces evil words from an evil heart. And I tell you this, that you must give an account on judgment day of every idle word you speak. The words you say now reflect your fate then; either you will be justified by them or you will be condemned."

Matthew 12:34–37

. . .

You cannot have Christian principles without Christ.

Dorothy L. Sayers

. . .

People can tame all kinds of animals and birds and reptiles and fish, but no one can tame the tongue. It is an uncontrollable evil, full of deadly poison. Sometimes it praises our Lord and Father, and sometimes it breaks out into curses against those who have been made in the image of God. And so blessing and cursing come pouring out of the same mouth. Surely, my brothers and sisters, this is not right! Gentle words bring life and health; a deceitful tongue crushes the spirit.

James 3:7–10; Proverbs 15:4

Dear children, let us stop just saying we love each other; let us really show it by our actions.

I John 3:18

Does a spring of water bubble out with both fresh water and bitter water? Can you pick olives from a fig tree or figs from a grapevine? No, and you can't draw fresh water from a salty pool. If you are wise and understand God's ways, live a life of steady goodness so that only good deeds will pour forth. And if you don't brag about the good you do, then you will be truly wise!

James 3:11–13

. . .

God has not always answered my prayers.
If he had,
I would have married the wrong man—
several times!

Ruth Bell Graham

. . .

Let your conversation be gracious and effective so that you will have the right answer for everyone.

Colossians 4:6

The wise person makes learning a joy; fools spout only foolishness.
Only the wise can give good advice; fools cannot do so.
A wise person is hungry for truth, while the fool feeds on trash.

Proverbs 15:2, 7, 14

Then watch your tongue! Keep your lips from telling lies!
Turn away from evil and do good. Work hard at living in peace with others.
The eyes of the LORD watch over those who do right; his ears are open to their cries for help.

Psalm 34:13–15

In everything you do, stay away from complaining and arguing, . . .behavior and deceit. Don't just pretend to be good! Be done with hypocrisy and jealousy and backstabbing. You must crave pure spiritual milk so that you can grow into the fullness of your salvation. Cry out for this nourishment as a baby cries for milk. So that no one can speak a word of blame against you. You are to live clean, innocent lives as children of God in a dark world full of crooked and perverse people. Let your lives shine brightly before them. Hold tightly to the word of life, so that when Christ returns, I will be proud that I did not lose the race and that my work was not useless.

Philippians 2:14; 1 Peter 2:1–2; Philippians 2:15–16

As long as I live, while I have breath from God, my lips will speak no evil, and my tongue will speak no lies.

Job 27:3–4

It is impossible to
mentally or socially enslave a
Bible—reading people.

—Horace Greeley

If you claim to be religious but don't control your tongue, you are just fooling yourself, and your religion is worthless. Hold on to the pattern of right teaching you learned from me. And remember to live in the faith and love that you have in Christ Jesus.

James 1:26; 2 Timothy 1:13

But in that coming day, no weapon turned against you will succeed. And everyone who tells lies in court will be brought to justice. These benefits are enjoyed by the servants of the LORD; their vindication will come from me. I, the LORD, have spoken!

Isaiah 54:17

"But I say, don't make any vows! If you say, 'By heaven!' It is a sacred vow because heaven is God's throne. And if you say, 'By the earth!' it is a sacred vow because the earth is his footstool. And don't swear, 'By Jerusalem!' For Jerusalem is the city of the great King. Don't even swear, 'By my head!' For you can't turn one hair white or black. Just say a simple, 'Yes, I will,' or 'No, I won't.' Your word is enough. To strengthen your promise with a vow shows that something is wrong."

Matthew 5:34–37

Prosperity

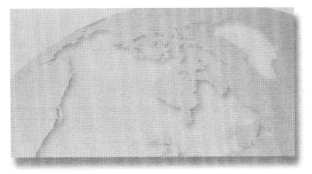

God! Thou art love! I build my faith on that!
I know thee, thou hast kept my path and made
Light for me in the darkness—tempering sorrow,
So that it reached me like a solemn joy;
It were too strange that I should doubt thy love.

—Robert Browning

And he will give you all you need from day to day if you live for him and make the Kingdom of God your primary concern.

Matthew 6:33

If you fully obey the LORD your God by keeping all the commands I am giving you today, the LORD your God will exalt you above all the nations of the world. You will experience all these blessings if you obey the LORD your God: You will be blessed in your towns and in the country. You will be blessed with many children and productive fields. You will be blessed with fertile herds and flocks. You will be blessed with baskets overflowing with fruit, and with kneading bowls filled with bread. You will be blessed wherever you go, both in coming and in going.

The LORD will bless everything you do and will fill your storehouses with grain. The LORD your God will bless you in the land he is giving you.

If you obey the commands of the LORD your God and walk in his ways, the LORD will establish you as his holy people as he solemnly promised to do.

The LORD will give you an abundance of good things in the land he swore to give your ancestors—many children, numerous livestock, and abundant crops. The LORD will send rain at the proper time from his rich treasury in the heavens to bless all the work you do. You will lend to many nations, but you will never need to borrow from them. If you listen to these commands of the LORD your God and carefully obey them, the LORD will make you the head and not the tail, and you will always have the upper hand. You must not turn away from any of the commands I am giving you today to follow after other gods and worship them.

Deuteronomy 28:1–6, 8–9, 11–14

"At that time you won't need to ask me for anything. The truth is, you can go directly to the Father and ask him, and he will grant your request because you use my name." Don't worry about anything; instead, pray about everything. Tell God what you need, and thank him for all he has done. And this same God who takes care of me will supply all your needs from his glorious riches, which have been given to us in Christ Jesus.

John 16:23; Philippians 4:6, 19

. . .

The Bible is like the poor; we have it always with us,
but we know very little about it.

Samuel Butler

. . .

Trust in the LORD and do good. Then you will live safely in the land and prosper.

Take delight in the LORD, and he will give you your heart's desires.

Commit everything you do to the LORD. Trust him, and he will help you.

He will make your innocence as clear as the dawn, and the justice of your cause will shine like the noonday sun.

Be still in the presence of the LORD, and wait patiently for him to act.

Psalm 37:3–7

"Beware! Don't be greedy for what you don't have. Real life is not measured by how much we own." Stay away from the love of money; be satisfied with what you have. For God has said, "I will never fail you. I will never forsake you."

Luke 12:15; Hebrews 13:5

. . .

One of the many divine qualities
of the Bible is this:
that it does not yield its secrets to
the irreverent and censorious.

J. I. Packer

. . .

Story of the Rich Fool

"A rich man had a fertile farm that produced fine crops. In fact, his barns were full to overflowing. So he said, 'I know! I'll tear down my barns and build bigger ones. Then I'll have room enough to store everything. And I'll sit back and say to myself, My friend, you have enough stored away for years to come. Now take it easy! Eat, drink, and be merry!'

"But God said to him, 'You fool! You will die this very night. Then who will get it all?'

"Yes, a person is a fool to store up earthly wealth but not have a rich relationship with God."

Luke 12:16–21

May your money perish with you for thinking God's gift can be bought! You can have no part in this, for your heart is not right before God. Turn from your wickedness and pray to the Lord. Perhaps he will forgive your evil thoughts.

Acts 8:20–22

"And how do you benefit if you gain the whole world but lose your own soul in the process? Is anything worth more than your soul? For I, the Son of Man, will come in the glory of my Father with his angels and will judge all people according to their deeds."

Matthew 16:26–27

"Should people cheat God? Yet you have cheated me! But you ask, 'When did we ever cheat you?'

"You have cheated me of the tithes and offerings due to me. You are under a curse, for your whole nation has been cheating me."

Malachi 3:8–9

"No one can serve two masters. For you will hate one and love the other, or be devoted to one and despise the other. You cannot serve both God and money."

Matthew 6:24

"Don't store up treasures here on earth, where they can be eaten by moths and get rusty, and where thieves break in and steal. Store your treasures in heaven, where they will never become moth-eaten or rusty and where they will be safe from thieves. Wherever your treasure is, there your heart and thoughts will also be."

Matthew 6:19–21

. . .

Building one's life on a foundation of gold
is just like building a house on
foundations of sand.

Henrik Ibsen

. . .

Remember this—a farmer who plants only a few seeds will get a small crop. But the one who plants generously will get a generous crop. You must each make up your own mind as to how much you should give. Don't give reluctantly or in response to pressure. For God loves the person who gives cheerfully.

2 Corinthians 9:6–7

Honor the LORD with your wealth and with the best part of everything your land produces. Then he will fill your barns with grain, and your vats will overflow with the finest wine.

Proverbs 3:9–10

It is better to be poor and honest than rich and crooked.

Proverbs 28:6

"If you give, you will receive. Your gift will return to you in full measure, pressed down, shaken together to make room for more, and running over. Whatever measure you use in giving—large or small—it will be used to measure what is given back to you."

Luke 6:38

And God will generously provide all you need. Then you will always have everything you need and plenty left over to share with others. Yes, you will be enriched so that you can give even more generously. And when we take your gifts to those who need them, they will break out in thanksgiving to God. Thank God for his Son—a gift too wonderful for words!

2 Corinthians 9:8, 11, 15

And it is a good thing to receive wealth from God and the good health to enjoy it. To enjoy your work and accept your lot in life—that is indeed a gift from God.

Ecclesiastes 5:19

Whatever is good and perfect comes to us from God above, who created all heaven's lights. Unlike them, he never changes or casts shifting shadows. For God's gifts and his call can never be withdrawn.

James 1:17; Romans 11:29

As the Scriptures say, "Godly people give generously to the poor. Their good deeds will never be forgotten." For God is the one who gives seed to the farmer and then bread to eat. In the same way, he will give you many opportunities to do good, and he will produce a great harvest of generosity in you.

2 Corinthians 9:9–10

. . .

If you make money your god,
it will plague you like the devil.

Henry Fielding

. . .

"Take care! Don't do your good deeds publicly, to be admired, because then you will lose the reward from your Father in heaven. When you give a gift to someone in need, don't shout about it as the hypocrites do—blowing trumpets in the synagogues and streets to call attention to their acts of charity! I assure you, they have received all the reward they will ever get. But when you give to someone, don't tell your left hand what your right hand is doing. Give your gifts in secret, and your Father, who knows all secrets, will reward you."

Matthew 6:1–4

Yet true religion with contentment is great wealth. After all, we didn't bring anything with us when we came into the world, and we certainly cannot carry anything with us when we die. So if we have enough food and clothing, let us be content. But people who long to be rich fall into temptation and are trapped by many foolish and harmful desires that plunge them into ruin and destruction. For the love of money is at the root of all kinds of evil. And some people, craving money, have wandered from the faith and pierced themselves with many sorrows. But you, Timothy, belong to God; so run from all these evil things, and follow what is right and good. Pursue a godly life, along with faith, love, perseverance, and gentleness.

I Timothy 6:6–11

Tell those who are rich in this world not to be proud and not to trust in their money, which will soon be gone. But their trust should be in the living God, who richly gives us all we need for our enjoyment. Tell them to use their money to do good. They should be rich in good works and should give generously to those in need, always being ready to share with others whatever God has given them. By doing this they will be storing up their treasure as a good foundation for the future so that they may take hold of real life.

Timothy, guard what God has entrusted to you. Avoid godless, foolish discussions with those who oppose you with their so-called knowledge.

I Timothy 6:17–20

"So I tell you, don't worry about everyday life—whether you have enough food, drink, and clothes. Doesn't life consist of more than food and clothing? Look at the birds. They don't need to plant or harvest or put food in barns because your heavenly Father feeds them. And you are far more valuable to him than they are. Can all your worries add a single moment to your life? Of course not.

"And why worry about your clothes? Look at the lilies and how they grow. They don't work or make their clothing. And if God cares so wonderfully for flowers that are here today and gone tomorrow, won't he more surely care for you? You have so little faith! Why be like the pagans who are so deeply concerned about these things? Your heavenly Father already knows all your needs, and he will give you all you need from day to day if you live for him and make the Kingdom of God your primary concern.

"So don't worry about tomorrow, for tomorrow will bring its own worries. Today's trouble is enough for today."

Matthew 6:25–28, 30, 32–34

"Bring all the tithes into the storehouse so there will be enough food in my Temple. If you do," says the LORD Almighty, "I will open the windows of heaven for you. I will pour out a blessing so great you won't have enough room to take it in! Try it! Let me prove it to you! Your crops will be abundant, for I will guard them from insects and disease. Your grapes will not shrivel before they are ripe," says the LORD Almighty.

Malachi 3:10–11

Money never made a man happy yet,
nor will it.
There is nothing in its nature
to produce happiness.
The more a man has, the more he wants.
Instead of its filling a vacuum,
it makes one.
If it satisfies one want,
it doubles and triples
that want another way.

—Benjamin Franklin

The Enemy

DEVIL, ADVERSARY, THIEF,
SATAN, DEVOURER,
GOD OF THIS WORLD,
WICKED ONE

There is nothing that Satan wants more
than to get good people in his sieve
and to sift them like wheat,
so that if possible he can
leave nothing but bran—
no grace, only the empty husk
and shell of religion.

—John Bunyan

The Fall of Satan

"How you are fallen from heaven, O shining star, son of the morning! You have been thrown down to the earth, you who destroyed the nations of the world. For you said to yourself, 'I will ascend to heaven and set my throne above God's stars.' I will preside on the mountain of the gods far away in the north. I will climb to the highest heavens and be like the Most High.' But instead, you will be brought down to the place of the dead, down to its lowest depths. Everyone there will stare at you and ask, 'Can this be the one who shook the earth and the kingdoms of the world? Is this the one who destroyed the world and made it into a wilderness? Is this the king who demolished the world's greatest cities and had no mercy on his prisoners?'"

Isaiah 14:12–17

Suddenly, I witnessed in heaven another significant event. I saw a large red dragon with seven heads and ten horns, with seven crowns on his heads. His tail dragged down one-third of the stars, which he threw to the earth. He stood before the woman as she was about to give birth to her child, ready to devour the baby as soon as it was born.

She gave birth to a boy who was to rule all nations with an iron rod. And the child was snatched away from the dragon and was caught up to God and to his throne.

Revelation 12:3–5

"You were in Eden, the garden of God. Your clothing was adorned with every precious stone—red carnelian, chrysolite, white moonstone, beryl, onyx, jasper, sapphire, turquoise, and emerald—all beautifully crafted for you and set in the finest gold. They were given to you on the day you were created. I ordained and anointed you as the mighty angelic guardian. You had access to the holy mountain of God and walked among the stones of fire.

"You were blameless in all you did from the day you were created until the day evil was found in you. Your great wealth filled you with violence, and you sinned. So I banished you from the mountain of God. I expelled you, O mighty guardian, from your place among the stones of fire. Your heart was filled with pride because of all your beauty. You corrupted your wisdom for the sake of your splendor. So I threw you to the earth and exposed you to the curious gaze of kings."

Ezekiel 28:13–17

War in Heaven

Then there was war in heaven. Michael and the angels under his command fought the dragon and his angels. And the dragon lost the battle and his angels. This great dragon—the ancient serpent called the Devil, or Satan, the one deceiving the whole world—was thrown down to the earth with all his angels.

Revelation 12:7–9

And I remind you of the angels who did not stay within the limits of authority God gave them but left the place where they belonged. God has kept them chained in prisons of darkness, waiting for the day of judgment.

Jude 1:6

. . .

We must not so much as taste of the devil's broth,
lest at last he brings us to eat of his beef.

Thomas Hall

. . .

But when people keep on sinning, it shows they belong to the Devil, who has been sinning since the beginning. But the Son of God came to destroy these works of the Devil.

1 John 3:8

If the Good News we preach is veiled from anyone, it is a sign that they are perishing. Satan, the God of this evil world, has blinded the minds of those who don't believe, so they are unable to see the glorious light of the Good News that is shining upon them. They don't understand the message we preach about the glory of Christ, who is the exact likeness of God.

2 Corinthians 4:3–4

Be careful! Watch out for attacks from the Devil, your great enemy. He prowls around like a roaring lion, looking for some victim to devour. Take a firm stand against him, and be strong in your faith. Remember that Christians all over the world are going through the same kind of suffering you are.

I Peter 5:8–9

So humble yourselves before God. Resist the Devil, and he will flee from you. Draw close to God, and God will draw close to you. Wash your hands, you sinners; purify your hearts, you hypocrites. So that Satan will not outsmart us. For we are very familiar with his evil schemes.

James 4:7–8; 2 Corinthians 2:11

"The thief's purpose is to steal and kill and destroy. My purpose is to give life in all its fullness."

John 10:10

And I will protect you from both your own people and the Gentiles. Yes, I am going to send you to the Gentiles, to open their eyes so they may turn from darkness to light, and from the power of Satan to God. Then they will receive forgiveness for their sins and be given a place among God's people, who are set apart by faith in me.

Acts 26:17–18

Then I heard a loud voice shouting across the heavens, "It has happened at last—the salvation and power and kingdom of our God, and the authority of his Christ! For the Accuser has been thrown down to earth—the one who accused our brothers and sisters before our God day and night. Rejoice, O heavens! And you who live in the heavens, rejoice! But terror will come on the earth and the sea. For the Devil has come down to you in great anger, and he knows that he has little time." And when the dragon realized that he had been thrown down to the earth, he pursued the woman who had given birth to the child. Then the dragon became angry at the woman, and he declared war against the rest of her children—all who keep God's commandments and confess that they belong to Jesus.

Revelation 12:10, 12–13, 17

"At last the time has come! . . . The Kingdom of God is near! Turn from your sins and believe this Good News! Beware of false prophets who come disguised as harmless sheep, but are really wolves that will tear you apart. For as the lightning lights up the entire sky, so it will be when the Son of Man comes. And he will send forth his angels with the sound of a mighty trumpet blast, and they will gather together his chosen ones from the farthest ends of the earth and heaven. Just so, when you see the events I've described beginning to happen, you can know his return is very near, right at the door."

Mark 1:15; Matthew 7:15; 24:27, 31, 33

THE ENEMY

And God will provide rest for you who are being persecuted and also for us when the Lord Jesus appears from heaven. He will come with his mighty angels, in flaming fire, bringing judgment on those who don't know God and on those who refuse to obey the Good News of our Lord Jesus.

2 Thessalonians 1:7–8

. . .

Satan fails to speak of the remorse,
the futility, the loneliness,
and the spiritual devastation which go
hand in hand with immorality.

Billy Graham

. . .

Don't be fooled by what they say. For that day will not come until there is a great rebellion against God and the man of lawlessness is revealed—the one who brings destruction. He will exalt himself and defy every god there is and tear down every object of adoration and worship. He will position himself in the temple of God, claiming that he himself is God.

2 Thessalonians 2:3–4

Devil:
the strongest and fiercest spirit
that fought in heaven,
now fiercer by despair.

—John Milton

And now in my vision I saw a beast rising up out of the sea. It had seven heads and ten horns, with ten crowns on its horns. And written on each head were names that blasphemed God. This beast looked like a leopard, but it had bear's feet and a lion's mouth! And the dragon gave him his own power and throne and great authority.

Then the beast was allowed to speak great blasphemies against God. And he was given authority to do what he wanted for forty-two months. Then I saw another beast come up out of the earth. He had two horns like those of a lamb, and he spoke with the voice of a dragon. He exercised all the authority of the first beast. And he required all the earth and those who belong to this world to worship the first beast, whose death-wound had been healed. And with all the miracles he was allowed to perform on behalf of the first beast, he deceived all the people who belong to this world. He ordered the people of the world to make a great statue of the first beast, who was fatally wounded and then came back to life.

His ten horns are ten kings who have not yet risen to power; they will be appointed to their kingdoms for one brief moment to reign with the beast. They will all agree to give their power and authority to him. Together they will wage war against the Lamb, but the Lamb will defeat them because he is Lord over all lords and King over all kings, and his people are the called and chosen and faithful ones.

Revelation 13:1–2, 5, 11, 12, 14; 17:12–14

Then the man of lawlessness will be revealed, whom the Lord Jesus will consume with the breath of his mouth and destroy by the splendor of his coming. This evil man will come to do the work of Satan with counterfeit power and signs and miracles. He will use every kind of wicked deception to fool those who are on their way to destruction because they refuse to believe the truth that would save them.

2 Thessalonians 2:8–10

. . .

Confusion is the dust raised by
the feet of the devil.

Frances J. Roberts

. . .

And the beast was captured, and with him the false prophet who did mighty miracles on behalf of the beast—miracles that deceived all who had accepted the mark of the beast and who worshiped his statue. Both the beast and his false prophet were thrown alive into the lake of fire that burns with sulfur.

Revelation 19:20

The beast you saw was alive but isn't now. And yet he will soon come up out of the bottomless pit and go to eternal destruction.

Revelation 17:8

Then I saw an angel come down from heaven with the key to the bottomless pit and a heavy chain in his hand. He seized the dragon—that old serpent, the Devil, Satan—and bound him in chains for a thousand years. The angel threw him into the bottomless pit, which he then shut and locked so Satan could not deceive the nations anymore until the thousand years were finished. Afterward he would be released again for a little while.

Then I saw thrones, and the people sitting on them had been given the authority to judge. And I saw the souls of those who had been beheaded for their testimony about Jesus, for proclaiming the word of God. And I saw the souls of those who had not worshiped the beast or his statue, nor accepted his mark on their forehead or their hands. They came to life again, and they reigned with Christ for a thousand years. This is the first resurrection. (The rest of the dead did not come back to life until the thousand years had ended.) Blessed and holy are those who share in the first resurrection. For them the second death holds no power, but they will be priests of God and of Christ and will reign with him a thousand years.

When the thousand years end, Satan will be let out of his prison. He will go out to deceive the nations from every corner of the earth, which are called Gog and Magog. He will gather them together for battle—a mighty host, as numberless as sand along the shore. And I saw them as they went up on the broad plain of the earth and surrounded God's people and the beloved city. But fire from heaven came down on the attacking armies and consumed them.

Then the Devil, who betrayed them, was thrown into the lake of fire that burns with sulfur, joining the beast and the false prophet. There they will be tormented day and night forever and ever.

Revelation 20:1–10

And he also said, "It is finished! I am the Alpha and the Omega—the Beginning and the End. To all who are thirsty I will give the springs of the water of life without charge! All who are victorious will inherit all these blessings, and I will be their God, and they will be my children."

Revelation 21:6–7

. . .

Christian love links love of God
and love of neighbor in a
twofold great commandment from which
neither element can be dropped,
so sin against neighbor through lack of
human love is sin against God.

Georgia Harkness

. . .

The whole world has now become the kingdom of our Lord and of his Christ, and he will reign forever and ever.

Revelation 11:15

The Mark of the Beast

He required everyone—great and small, rich and poor, slave and free—to be given a mark on the right hand or on the forehead. And no one could buy or sell anything without that mark, which was either the name of the beast or the number representing his name. Wisdom is needed to understand this. Let the one who has understanding solve the number of the beast, for it is the number of a man. His number is 666.

Revelation 13:16–18

Anyone who worships the beast and his statue or who accepts his mark on the forehead or the hand must drink the wine of God's wrath. It is poured out undiluted into God's cup of wrath. And they will be tormented with fire and burning sulfur in the presence of the holy angels and the Lamb. The smoke of their torment rises forever and ever, and they will have no relief day or night, for they have worshiped the beast and his statue and have accepted the mark of his name.

Revelation 14:9–11

But cowards who turn away from me, and unbelievers, and the corrupt, and murderers, and the immoral, and those who practice witchcraft, and idol worshipers, and all liars—their doom is in the lake that burns with fire and sulfur. This is the second death.

Revelation 21:8

For a thing to be satanic does not mean that
it is abominable and immoral;
the satanically-managed man is
absolutely self-governed and
has no need of God.

—Oswald Chambers

Sin

The infernal serpent;
he it was, whose guile,
Stirred up with envy
and revenge, deceived
The mother of mankind.

—John Milton

The Scriptures tell us. "The first man, Adam, became a living person." But the last Adam—that is, Christ—is a life-giving Spirit. What came first was the natural body, then the spiritual body comes later. Adam, the first man, was made from the dust of the earth, while Christ, the second man, came from heaven. Every human being has an earthly body just like Adam's, but our heavenly bodies will be just like Christ's. Just as we are now like Adam, the man of the earth, so we will someday be like Christ, the man from heaven.

I Corinthians 15:45–49

When Adam sinned, sin entered the entire human race. Adam's sin brought death, so death spread to everyone, for everyone sinned. They all died anyway—even though they did not disobey an explicit commandment of God, as Adam did. What a contrast between Adam and Christ, who was yet to come! The sin of this one man, Adam caused death to rule over us, but all who receive God's wonderful, gracious gift of righteousness will live in triumph over sin and death through this one man, Jesus Christ.

Yes, Adam's one sin brought condemnation upon everyone, but Christ's one act of righteousness makes all people right in God's sight and gives them life. Because one person disobeyed God, many people became sinners. But because one other person obeyed God, many people will be made right in God's sight.

Romans 5:12, 14, 17–19

Sin Unto Death

I say this because some godless people have wormed their way in among you, saying that God's forgiveness allows us to live immoral lives. The fate of such people was determined long ago, for they have turned against our only Master and Lord, Jesus Christ.

Jude 1:4

. . .

Wanderer, come,
there's room for thee,
At the cross of Jesus;
Come and taste salvation free
At the Cross of Jesus.

Fanny Crosby

. . .

Yes, they knew God, but they wouldn't worship him as God or even give him thanks. And they began to think up foolish ideas of what God was like. The result was that their minds became dark and confused.

Claiming to be wise, they became utter fools instead. That is why God abandoned them to their shameful desires. Even the women turned against the natural way to have sex and instead indulged in sex with each other. And the men, instead of having normal sexual relationships with women, burned with lust for each other. Men did shameful things with other men and, as a result, suffered within themselves the penalty they so richly deserved.

Their lives became full of every kind of wickedness, sin, greed, hate, envy, murder, fighting, deception, malicious behavior, and gossip. They are backstabbers, haters of God, insolent, proud, and boastful. They are forever inventing new ways of sinning and are disobedient to their parents. They refuse to understand, break their promises, and are heartless and unforgiving. They are fully aware of God's death penalty for those who do these things, yet they go right ahead and do them anyway. And, worse yet, they encourage others to do them, too.

You may be saying, "What terrible people you have been talking about!" But you are just as bad, and you have no excuse! When you say they are wicked and should be punished, you are condemning yourself, for you do these very same things.

Romans 1:21–22, 26–27, 29–2:1

"A tree is identified by its fruit. Make a tree good, and its fruit will be good. Make a tree bad, and its fruit will be bad."

Matthew 12:33

And don't forget the cities of Sodom and Gomorrah and their neighboring towns, which were filled with sexual immorality and every kind of sexual perversion. Those cities were destroyed by fire and are a warning of the eternal fire that will punish all who are evil.

Jude 1:7

We must not be like Cain, who belonged to the evil one and killed his brother. And why did he kill him? Because Cain had been doing what was evil, and his brother had been doing what was right.

1 John 3:12

Don't you realize that whatever you choose to obey becomes your master? You can choose sin, which leads to death, or you can choose to obey God and receive his approval. Now you are free from sin, your old master, and you have become slaves to your new master, righteousness.

Romans 6:16, 18

Yet these false teachers, who claim authority from their dreams, live immoral lives, defy authority, and scoff at the power of the glorious ones. But these people mock and curse the things they do not understand. Like animals, they do whatever their instincts tell them, and they bring about their own destruction. How terrible it will be for them! For they follow the evil example of Cain, who killed his brother. Like Balaam, they will do anything for money. And like Korah, they will perish because of their rebellion.

Jude 1:8, 10–11

"I assure you that everyone who sins is a slave of sin. I am telling you what I saw when I was with my Father. But you are following the advice of your father. No, you are obeying your real father when you act that way. For you are the children of your father the Devil, and you love to do the evil things he does. He was a murderer from the beginning and has always hated the truth. There is no truth in him. When he lies, it is consistent with his character; for he is a liar and the father of lies. Anyone whose Father is God listens gladly to the words of God. Since you don't, it proves you aren't God's children."

John 8:34, 38, 41, 44, 47

. . .

It is so stupid of modern civilization
to have given up belief in
the devil when he is
the only explanation of it.

Ronald Knox

. . .

Let the people turn from their wicked deeds. Let them banish from their minds the very thought of doing wrong! Let them turn to the LORD that he may have mercy on them. Yes, turn to our God, for he will abundantly pardon.

Isaiah 55:7

Temptation

"Keep alert and pray. Otherwise temptation will overpower you. For though the spirit is willing enough, the body is weak!"

Matthew 26:41

. . .

God delights in our temptations
and yet hates them,
He delights in them when they drive us to prayer;
he hates them when they drive us to despair.

Martin Luther

. . .

And remember, no one who wants to do wrong should ever say, "God is tempting me." God is never tempted to do wrong, and he never tempts anyone else either. Temptation comes from the lure of our own evil desires. These evil desires lead to evil actions, and evil actions lead to death. So don't be misled, my dear brothers and sisters. For the wages of sin is death, but the free gift of God is eternal life through Christ Jesus our Lord.

James 1:13–16; Romans 6:23

But remember that the temptations that come into your life are no different from what others experience. And God is faithful. He will keep the temptation from becoming so strong that you can't stand up against it. When you are tempted, he will show you a way out so that you will not give in to it.

1 Corinthians 10:13

So you see, the Lord knows how to rescue godly people from their trials, even while punishing the wicked right up until the day of judgment.

2 Peter 2:9

For God did not spare even the angels when they sinned; he threw them into hell, in gloomy caves and darkness until the judgment day. And God did not spare the ancient world—except for Noah and his family of seven. Noah warned the world of God's righteous judgment. Then God destroyed the whole world of ungodly people with a vast flood. Later, he turned the cities of Sodom and Gomorrah into heaps of ashes and swept them off the face of the earth. He made them an example of what will happen to ungodly people. But at the same time, God rescued Lot out of Sodom because he was a good man who was sick of all the immorality and wickedness around him. Yes, he was a righteous man who was distressed by the wickedness he saw and heard day after day.

2 Peter 2:4–8

Jesus Christ is the same yesterday, today, and forever.

Hebrews 13:8

Remember, it is better to suffer for doing good, if that is what God wants, than to suffer for doing wrong! So if you are suffering according to God's will, keep on doing what is right, and trust yourself to the God who made you, for he will never fail you.

I Peter 3:17; 4:19

. . .

God did not abolish the fact of evil;
he transformed it.
He did not stop the Crucifixion;
he rose from the dead.

Dorothy L. Sayers

. . .

Stop loving this evil world and all that it offers you, for when you love the world, you show that you do not have the love of the Father in you. For the world offers only the lust for physical pleasure, the lust for everything we see, and pride in our possessions. These are not from the Father. They are from this evil world. And this world is fading away, along with everything it craves. But if you do the will of God, you will live forever.

I John 2:15–17

We know that those who have become part of God's family do not make a practice of sinning, for God's Son holds them securely, and the evil one cannot get his hands on them.

I John 5:18

I am warning you ahead of time, dear friends, so that you can watch out and not be carried away by the errors of these wicked people. I don't want you to lose your own secure footing. But grow in the special favor and knowledge of our Lord and Savior Jesus Christ.

2 Peter 3:17–18

Therefore, since we are surrounded by such a huge crowd of witnesses to the life of faith, let us strip off every weight that slows us down, especially the sin that so easily hinders our progress. And let us run with endurance the race that God has set before us. We do this by keeping our eyes on Jesus, on whom our faith depends from start to finish. He was willing to die a shameful death on the cross because of the joy he knew would be his afterward. Now he is seated in the place of highest honor beside God's throne in heaven. Think about all he endured when sinful people did such terrible things to him, so that you don't become weary and give up.

Hebrews 12:1–3

Salvation

A person may go to heaven without health,
without riches, without honors,
without leaning, without friends;
but he can never go there
without Christ.

—John Dyer

And every tongue will confess that Jesus Christ is Lord, to the glory of God the Father. Dearest friends, you were always so careful to follow my instructions when I was with you. And now that I am away you must be even more careful to put into action God's saving work in your lives, obeying God with deep reverence and fear.

Philippians 2:11–12

But if we confess our sins to him, he is faithful and just to forgive us and to cleanse us from every wrong. My dear children, I am writing this to you so that you will not sin. But if you do sin, there is someone to plead for you before the Father. He is Jesus Christ, the one who pleases God completely. He died for our sins, just as God our Father planned, in order to rescue us from this evil world in which we live.

1 John 1:9; 2:1; Galatians 1:4

So even though Jesus was God's Son, he learned obedience from the things he suffered. In this way, God qualified him as a perfect High Priest, and he became the source of eternal salvation for all those who obey him.

Hebrews 5:8–9

For if you confess with your mouth that Jesus is Lord and believe in your heart that God raised him from the dead, you will be saved. For it is by believing in your heart that you are made right with God, and it is by confessing with your mouth that you are saved.

Romans 10:9–10

For the Scriptures say, "'As surely as I live,' says the Lord, 'every knee will bow to me and every tongue will confess allegiance to God.'" Yes, each of us will have to give a personal account to God.

Romans 14:11–12

Have mercy on me, O God, because of your unfailing love. Because of your great compassion, blot out the stain of my sins. Wash me clean from my guilt. Purify me from my sin. For I recognize my shameful deeds—they haunt me day and night. Create in me a clean heart, O God. Renew a right spirit within me.

Psalm 51:1–3, 10

. . .

For a cap and bells our lives we pay,
Bubbles we buy with a whole soul's tasking:
'Tis heaven alone that is given away,
'tis only God may be had for the asking.

James Russell Lowell

. . .

"Anyone who believes and is baptized will be saved. But anyone who refuses to believe will be condemned."

Mark 16:16

For I am not ashamed of this Good News about Christ. It is the power of God at work, saving everyone who believes—Jews first and also Gentiles. This Good News tells us how God makes us right in his sight. This is accomplished from start to finish by faith. As the Scriptures say, "It is through faith that a righteous person has life."

Romans 1:16–17

. . .

Just as Christian came up with the cross,
his burden loosed from off his shoulders
and fell from off his back
and began to tumble,
and so continued to do till it
came to the mouth of the sepulcher,
where it fell in,
and I saw it no more.

John Bunyan

. . .

Don't you realize that all of you together are the temple of God and that the Spirit of God lives in you?

1 Corinthians 3:16

Another reason for right living is that you know how late it is; time is running out. Wake up, for the coming of our salvation is nearer now than when we first believed. The night is almost gone; the day of salvation will soon be here. So don't live in darkness. Get rid of your evil deeds. Shed them like dirty clothes. Clothe yourselves with the armor of right living, as those who live in the light. We should be decent and true in everything we do, so that everyone can approve of our behavior. Don't participate in wild parties and getting drunk, or in adultery and immoral living, or in fighting and jealousy. But let the Lord Jesus Christ take control of you, and don't think of ways to indulge your evil desires.

Romans 13:11–14

"I assure you, unless you are born again, you can never see the Kingdom of God. The truth is, no one can enter the Kingdom of God without being born of water and the Spirit. Humans can reproduce only human life, but the Holy Spirit gives new life from heaven. So don't be surprised at my statement that you must be born again."

John 3:3, 5–7

For God has reserved a priceless inheritance for his children. It is kept in heaven for you, pure and undefiled, beyond the reach of change and decay. Because we have these promises, dear friends, let us cleanse ourselves from everything that can defile our body or spirit. And let us work toward complete purity because we fear God.

1 Peter 1:4; 2 Corinthians 7:1

All who proclaim that Jesus is the Son of God have God living in them, and they live in God. We know how much God loves us, and we have put our trust in him.

God is love, and all who live in love live in God, and God lives in them. And as we live in God, our love grows more perfect. So we will not be afraid on the day of judgment, but we can face him with confidence because we are like Christ here in this world.

1 John 4:15–17

Now you can have sincere love for each other as brothers and sisters because you were cleansed from your sins when you accepted the truth of the Good News. So see to it that you really do love each other intensely with all your hearts.

For you have been born again. Your new life did not come from your earthly parents because the life they gave you will end in death. But this new life will last forever because it comes from the eternal, living word of God. For every child of God defeats this evil world by trusting Christ to give the victory.

1 Peter 1:22–23; 1 John 5:4

All of these things are for your benefit. And as God's grace brings more and more people to Christ, there will be great thanksgiving, and God will receive more and more glory.

That is why we never give up. Though our bodies are dying, our spirits are being renewed every day.

2 Corinthians 4:15–16

And so, dear Christian friends, I plead with you to give your bodies to God. Let them be a living and holy sacrifice—the kind he will accept. When you think of what he has done for you, is this too much to ask? Don't copy the behavior and customs of this world, but let God transform you into a new person by changing the way you think. Then you will know what God wants you to do, and you will know how good and pleasing and perfect his will really is.

Romans 12:1–2

. . .

It is a profound irony that
the Son of God visited this planet,
and one of the chief complaints
against him was
that he was not religious enough.

Rebecca Pippert

. . .

Let the people turn from their wicked deeds. Let them banish from their minds the very thought of doing wrong! Let them turn to the LORD that he may have mercy on them. Yes, turn to our God, for he will abundantly pardon.

Isaiah 55:7

Look! Here I stand at the door and knock. If you hear me calling and open the door, I will come in, and we will share a meal as friends. I will invite everyone who is victorious to sit with me on my throne, just as I was victorious and sat with my Father on his throne.

Revelation 3:20–21

To all who are thirsty I will give the springs of the water of life without charge! All who are victorious will inherit all these blessings, and I will be their God, and they will be my children.

Revelation 21:6–7

Satisfy us in the morning with your unfailing love, so we may sing for joy to the end of our lives. Give us gladness in proportion to our former misery! Replace the evil years with good. Let us see your miracles again; let our children see your glory at work.

Psalm 90:14–16

But the love of the LORD remains forever with those who fear him. His salvation extends to the children's children of those who are faithful to his covenant, of those who obey his commandments!

Psalm 103:17–18

He rescues and saves his people; he performs miraculous signs and wonders in the heavens and on earth.

Daniel 6:27

Sin separates,
pain isolates,
but salvation and
comfort unite.

—Julian of Norwich

As for God, his way is perfect. All the LORD's promises prove true. He is a shield for all who look to him for protection. God arms me with strength; he has made my way safe.

Psalm 18:30, 32

This I declare of the LORD: He alone is my refuge, my place of safety; he is my God, and I am trusting him. For he will rescue you from every trap and protect you from the fatal plague. He will shield you with his wings. He will shelter you with his feathers. His faithful promises are your armor and protection. Do not be afraid of the terrors of the night, nor fear the dangers of the day, nor dread the plague that stalks in darkness, nor the disaster that strikes at midday.

Though a thousand fall at your side, though ten thousand are dying around you, these evils will not touch you. But you will see it with your eyes; you will see how the wicked are punished.

If you make the LORD your refuge, if you make the Most High your shelter, no evil will conquer you; no plague will come near your dwelling. For he orders his angels to protect you wherever you go. They will hold you with their hands to keep you from striking your foot on a stone. You will trample down lions and poisonous snakes; you will crush fierce lions and serpents under your feet!

Psalm 91:2–13

I write this to you who believe in the Son of God, so that you may know you have eternal life.

1 John 5:13

Prayer and Supplication

It is only when men begin to worship
that they begin to grow.

—Calvin Coolidge

I urge you, first of all, to pray for all people. As you make your requests, plead for God's mercy upon them, and give thanks. Pray this way for kings and all others who are in authority, so that we can live in peace and quietness, in godliness and dignity. This is good and pleases God our Savior, for he wants everyone to be saved and to understand the truth.

1 Timothy 2:1–4

A final word: Be strong with the Lord's mighty power. Put on all of God's armor so that you will be able to stand firm against all strategies and tricks of the Devil. For we are not fighting against people made of flesh and blood, but against the evil rulers and authorities of the unseen world, against those mighty powers of darkness who rule this world, and against wicked spirits in the heavenly realms. Put on salvation as your helmet, and take the sword of the Spirit, which is the word of God. Pray at all times and on every occasion in the power of the Holy Spirit. Stay alert and be persistent in your prayers for all Christians everywhere.

Ephesians 6:10–12; 17–18

Don't worry about anything; instead, pray about everything. Tell God what you need, and thank him for all he has done. If you do this, you will experience God's peace, which is far more wonderful than the human mind can understand. His peace will guard your hearts and minds as you live in Christ Jesus. And this same God who takes care of me will supply all your needs from his glorious riches, which have been given to us in Christ Jesus.

Philippians 4:6–7, 19

So we have continued praying for you ever since we first heard about you. We ask God to give you a complete understanding of what he wants to do in your lives, and we ask him to make you wise with spiritual wisdom. Then the way you live will always honor and please the Lord, and you will continually do good, kind things for others. All the while, you will learn to know God better and better.

We also pray that you will be strengthened with his glorious power so that you will have all the patience and endurance you need. May you be filled with joy, always thanking the Father, who has enabled you to share the inheritance that belongs to God's holy people, who live in the light.

Colossians 1:9–12

I have never stopped thanking God for you. I pray for you constantly, asking God, the glorious Father of our Lord Jesus Christ, to give you spiritual wisdom and understanding, so that you might grow in your knowledge of God. I pray that your hearts will be flooded with light so that you can understand the wonderful future he has promised to those he called. I want you to realize what a rich and glorious inheritance he has given to his people.

I pray that you will begin to understand the incredible greatness of his power for us who believe him. This is the same mighty power that raised Christ from the dead.

Ephesians 1:16–20

"Listen to me! You can pray for anything, and if you believe, you will have it."

Mark 11:24

Learn to be wise, and develop good judgment. Don't forget or turn away from my words. Getting wisdom is the most important thing you can do! And whatever else you do, get good judgment.

Proverbs 4:5, 7

. . .

There is no neutral ground in the universe:
every square inch, every split second,
is claimed by God
and counterclaimed by Satan.

C. S. Lewis

. . .

Devote yourselves to prayer with an alert mind and a thankful heart. Live wisely among those who are not Christians, and make the most of every opportunity.

Colossians 4:2, 5

"But when you are praying, first forgive anyone you are holding a grudge against, so that your Father in heaven will forgive your sins, too. But if you do not forgive, neither will your Father who is in heaven forgive your sins."

Mark 11:25–26

"But when you pray, go away by yourself, shut the door behind you, and pray to your Father secretly. Then your Father, who knows all secrets, will reward you.

"When you pray, don't babble on and on as people of other religions do. They think their prayers are answered only by repeating their words again and again. Don't be like them, because your Father knows exactly what you need even before you ask him!"

Matthew 6:6–8

. . .

The worship of God is not a rule of safety—
it is an adventure of the spirit.

Alfred North Whitehead

. . .

If you need wisdom—if you want to know what God wants you to do—ask him, and he will gladly tell you. He will not resent your asking. But when you ask him, be sure that you really expect him to answer, for a doubtful mind is as unsettled as a wave of the sea that is driven and tossed by the wind. People like that should not expect to receive anything from the Lord. They can't make up their minds. They waver back and forth in everything they do.

James 1:5–8

You want what you don't have, so you scheme and kill to get it. You are jealous for what others have, and you can't possess it, so you fight and quarrel to take it away from them. And yet the reason you don't have what you want is that you don't ask God for it. And even when you do ask, you don't get it because your whole motive is wrong—you want only what will give you pleasure.

James 4:2–3

"Keep on asking, and you will be given what you ask for. Keep on looking, and you will find. Keep on knocking, and the door will be opened. For everyone who asks, receives. Everyone who seeks, finds. And the door is opened to everyone who knocks. I assure you, if you have faith and don't doubt, you can do things like this and much more. You can even say to this mountain, 'May God lift you up and throw you into the sea,' and it will happen. If you believe, you will receive whatever you ask for in prayer."

Matthew 7:7–8; 21:21–22

That is why we have a great High Priest who has gone to heaven, Jesus the Son of God. Let us cling to him and never stop trusting him. This High Priest of ours understands our weaknesses, for he faced all of the same temptations we do, yet he did not sin So let us come boldly to the throne of our gracious God. There we will receive his mercy, and we will find grace to help us when we need it.

Hebrews 4:14–16

"Keep alert and pray. Otherwise temptation will overpower you. For though the spirit is willing enough, the body is weak."

Mark 14:38

I pray that your love for each other will overflow more and more, and that you will keep on growing in your knowledge and understanding. For I want you to understand what really matters, so that you may live pure and blameless lives until Christ returns. May you always be filled with the fruit of your salvation—those good things that are produced in your life by Jesus Christ—for this will bring much glory and praise to God.

Philippians 1:9–11

The end of the world is coming soon. Therefore, be earnest and disciplined in your prayers. Most important of all, continue to show deep love for each other, for love covers a multitude of sins. "And since you don't know when that will happen, stay alert and keep watch."

1 Peter 4:7–8; Mark 13:33

Keep on praying. No matter what happens, always be thankful, for this is God's will for you who belong to Christ Jesus.

1 Thessalonians 5:17–18

Prayer enlarges the heart until
it is capable of containing
God's gift of himself.

—Mother Teresa of Calcutta

Healing

To God be the glory, great things he has done;
So loved he the world that he gave us his Son,
Who yielded his life and atonement for sin,
And opened the life gate that all may go in.

—Fanny Crosby

But Christ has rescued us from the curse pronounced by the law. When he was hung on the cross, he took upon himself the curse for our wrongdoing. For it is written in the Scriptures, "Cursed is everyone who is hung on a tree." Through the work of Christ Jesus, God has blessed the Gentiles with the same blessing he promised to Abraham, and we Christians receive the promised Holy Spirit through faith. He personally carried away our sins in his own body on the cross so we can be dead to sin and live for what is right. You have been healed by his wounds!

Galatians 3:13–14; 1 Peter 2:24

. . .

Sometimes the Lord disturbs the waters
before sending his healing angel.

John Harper

. . .

And no doubt you know that God anointed Jesus of Nazareth with the Holy Spirit and with power. Then Jesus went around doing good and healing all who were oppressed by the Devil, for God was with him. That evening many demon-possessed people were brought to Jesus. All the spirits fled when he commanded them to leave; and he healed all the sick. This fulfilled the word of the Lord through Isaiah, who said, "He took our sicknesses and removed our diseases."

Acts. 10:38; Matthew 8:16–17

"Yes, I came from the Father into the world, and I will leave the world and return to the Father. I have told you all this so that you may have peace in me. Here on earth you will have many trials and sorrows. But take heart, because I have overcome the world."

John 16:28, 33

He was oppressed and treated harshly, yet he never said a word. He was led as a lamb to the slaughter. And as a sheep is silent before the shearers, he did not open his mouth. He had done no wrong, and he never deceived anyone. But he was buried like a criminal; he was put in a rich man's grave.

But it was the LORD's good plan to crush him and fill him with grief. Yet when his life is made an offering for sin, he will have a multitude of children, many heirs. He will enjoy a long life, and the LORD's plan will prosper in his hands. When he sees all that is accomplished by his anguish, he will be satisfied. And because of what he has experienced, my righteous servant will make it possible for many to be counted righteous, for he will bear all their sins. I will give him the honors of one who is mighty and great, because he exposed himself to death. He was counted among those who were sinners. He bore the sins of many and interceded for sinners. He was despised and rejected—a man of sorrows, acquainted with bitterest grief. We turned our backs on him and looked the other way when he went by. He was despised and we did not care. But he was wounded and crushed for our sins. He was beaten that we might have peace. He was whipped, and we were healed!

Isaiah 53:7, 9–12; 53:3, 5

"I have been given complete authority in heaven and on earth. And I have given you authority over all the power of the enemy. Therefore, go and make disciples of all the nations, baptizing them in the name of the Father and the Son and the Holy Spirit. Teach these new disciples to obey all the commands I have given you. And be sure of this: I am with you always, even to the end of the age."

Matthew 28:18; Luke 10:19; Matthew 28:19–20

"You haven't done this before. Ask, using my name, and you will receive, and you will have abundant joy. At that time you won't need to ask me for anything. The truth is, you can go directly to the Father and ask him, and he will grant your request because you use my name. Then you will ask in my name. But the time is soon coming when I , the Son of Man, will be sitting at God's right hand in the place of power."

John 16:24, 23, 26; Luke 22:69

That is why we have a great High Priest who has gone to heaven, Jesus the Son of God. Let us cling to him and never stop trusting him. So let us come boldly to the throne of our gracious God. There we will receive his mercy, and we will find grace to help us when we need it.

Hebrews 4:14, 16

"I tell you this: Whatever you prohibit on earth is prohibited in heaven, and whatever you allow on earth is allowed in heaven. Do you believe I can make you see? . . . Because of your faith, it will happen."

Matthew 18:18; 9:28–29

"Anyone who believes and is baptized will be saved. But anyone who refuses to believe will be condemned. These signs will accompany those who believe: They will cast out demons in my name, and they will speak new languages. . . . They will be able to place their hands on the sick and heal them."

Mark 16:16–18

. . .

Blessed Redeemer, wonderful Savior,
Fountain of wisdom, Ancient of Days,
Hope of the faithful, Light of all ages,
Jesus my Savior, thee will I praise.

Fanny Crosby

. . .

Are any among you suffering? They should keep on praying about it. And those who have reason to be thankful should continually sing praises to the Lord.

Are any among you sick? They should call for the elders of the church and have them pray over them, anointing them with oil in the name of the Lord. And their prayer offered in faith will heal the sick, and the Lord will make them well. And anyone who has committed sins will be forgiven.

James 5:13–15

"I also tell you this: If two of you agree down here on earth concerning anything you ask, my Father in heaven will do it for you. For where two or three gather together because they are mine, I am there among them."

Matthew 18:19–20

Confess your sins to each other and pray for each other so that you may be healed. The earnest prayer of a righteous person has great power and wonderful results.

James 5:16

. . .

The whole point of this life is the healing of the heart's eye through which God is seen.

Augustine of Hippo

. . .

And the Holy Spirit helps us in our distress. For we don't even know what we should pray for, nor how we should pray. But the Holy Spirit prays for us with groanings that cannot be expressed in words. And the Father who knows all hearts knows what the Spirit is saying, for the Spirit pleads for us believers in harmony with God's own will.

Romans 8:26–27

The LORD hears his people when they call to him for help. He rescues them from all their troubles. The righteous face many troubles, but the LORD rescues them from each and every one.

Psalm 34:17, 19

Pay attention, my child, to what I say. Listen carefully. Don't lose sight of my words. Let them penetrate deep within your heart, for they bring life and radiant health to anyone who discovers their meaning.

Above all else, guard your heart, for it affects everything you do.

Proverbs 4:20–23

Then if my people who are called by my name will humble themselves and pray and seek my face and turn from their wicked ways, I will hear from heaven and will forgive their sins and heal their land. I will listen to every prayer made in this place.

2 Chronicles 7:14–15

Seek his will in all you do, and he will direct your paths.

Don't be impressed with your own wisdom. Instead, fear the LORD and turn your back on evil. Then you will gain renewed health and vitality.

Proverbs 3:6–8

Anointing

What built St. Paul's Cathedral?
Look at the heart of the matter,
it was that divine Hebrew book—
the word partly of the man,
Moses, an outlaw
tending his Midianitish herds, four thousand
years ago,
in the wilderness of Sinai!
It is the strangest of things,
yet nothing is truer.

—Thomas Carlyle

And no doubt you know that God anointed Jesus of Nazareth with the Holy Spirit and with power. Then Jesus went around doing good and healing all who were oppressed by the Devil, for God was with him.

Acts 10:38

But you have received the Holy Spirit, and he lives within you, so you don't need anyone to teach you what is true. For the Spirit teaches you all things, and what he teaches is true—it is not a lie. So continue in what he has taught you, and continue to live in Christ.

1 John 2:27

. . .

If we seek God
for our own good and profit,
we are not seeking God.

Meister Eckahrt

. . .

And now, just as you accepted Christ Jesus as your Lord, you must continue to live in obedience to him. Let your roots grow down into him and draw up nourishment from him, so you will grow in faith, strong and vigorous in the truth you were taught. Let your lives overflow with thanksgiving, for all he has done.

Colossians 2:6–7

"You didn't choose me, I chose you. I appointed you to go and produce fruit that will last, so that the Father will give you whatever you ask for, using my name."

John 15:16

"I am the true vine, and my Father is the gardener. Yes, I am the vine; you are the branches. Those who remain in me, and I in them, will produce much fruit. For apart from me you can do nothing. But if you stay joined to me and my words remain in you, you may ask any request you like, and it will be granted!

John 15:1, 5, 7

For all of God's promises have been fulfilled in him. That is why we say, "Amen" when we give glory to God through Christ. It is God who gives us, along with you, the ability to stand firm for Christ. He has commissioned us, and he has identified us as his own by placing the Holy Spirit in our hearts as the first installment of everything he will give us.

2 Corinthians 1:20–22

So, dear friends, work hard to prove that you really are among those God has called and chosen. Doing this, you will never stumble or fall away. You should continue on as you were when God called you. God purchased you at a high price. Don't be enslaved by the world. So, dear brothers and sisters, whatever situation you were in when you became a believer, stay there in your new relationship with God.

2 Peter 1:10; 1 Corinthians 7:20, 23–24

For we are God's masterpiece. He has created us anew in Christ Jesus, so that we can do the good things he planned for us long ago.

Ephesians 2:10

For God is working in you, giving you the desire to obey him and the power to do what pleases him. It is God who saved us and chose us to live a holy life. He did this not because we deserved it, but because that was his plan long before the world began—to show his love and kindness to us through Christ Jesus. And now he has made all of this plain to us by the coming of Christ Jesus, our Savior, who broke the power of death and showed us the way to everlasting life through the Good News.

Philippians 2:13; 2 Timothy 1:9–10

May our Lord Jesus Christ and God our Father, who loved us and in his special favor gave us everlasting comfort and good hope, comfort your hearts and give you strength in every good thing you do and say.

2 Thessalonians 2:16–17

And we know that God causes everything to work together for the good of those who love God and are called according to his purpose for them. And having chosen them, he called them to come to him. And he gave them right standing with himself, and he promised them his glory.

Romans 8:28, 30

Or don't you know that your body is the temple of the Holy Spirit, who lives in you and was given to you by God? You do not belong to yourself, for God bought you with a high price. So you must honor God with your body.

1 Corinthians 6:19–20

And what union can there be between God's temple and idols? For we are the temple of the living God. As God said: "I will live in them and walk among them. I will be their God, and they will be my people."

2 Corinthians 6:16

. . .

I have found in the Bible
words for my inmost thoughts,
songs for my joy,
utterance for my hidden griefs
and pleadings for my shame and feebleness.

Samuel Taylor Coleridge

. . .

The Spirit of God, who raised Jesus from the dead, lives in you. And just as he raised Christ from the dead, he will give life to your mortal body by this same Spirit living within you.

Romans 8:11

And God will raise our bodies from the dead by his marvelous power, just as he raised our Lord from the dead. Don't you realize that your bodies are actually parts of Christ?

I Corinthians 6:14–15

And I am sure that God, who began the good work within you, will continue his work until it is finally finished on the day when Christ Jesus comes back again.

Philippians 1:6

. . .

God's gifts put man's best dreams to shame.

Elizabeth Barrett Browning

. . .

Keep putting into practice all you learned from me and heard from me and saw me doing, and the God of peace will be with you.

Philippians 4:9

If someone says, "I belong to God," but doesn't obey God's commandments, that person is a liar and does not live in the truth. But those who obey God's word really do love him. That is the way to know whether or not we live in him. Those who say they live in God should live their lives as Christ did.

I John 2:4–6

Stewardship

If a man is called to be
a street sweeper he should sweep streets
even as Michelangelo painted,
or Beethoven composed music.
He should sweep streets so well that
all the host of heaven and earth
will pause and say,
here lived a great street sweeper
who did his job well.

—Martin Luther King, Jr.

As for God, his way is perfect. All the LORD's promises prove true. He is a shield for all who look to him for protection. God arms me with strength; he has made my way safe. For I can do everything with the help of Christ who gives me the strength I need.

Psalm 18:30, 32; Philippians 4:13

What this means is that those who become Christians become new persons. They are not the same anymore, for the old life is gone. A new life has begun!

2 Corinthians 5:17

Now, a person who is put in charge as a manager must be faithful. We have worked wearily with our own hands to earn our living. We bless those who curse us. We are patient with those who abuse us. If you are a thief, stop stealing. Begin using your hands for honest work, and then give generously to others in need.

1 Corinthians 4:2, 12; Ephesians 4:28

But there is going to come a time of testing at the judgment day to see what kind of work each builder has done. Everyone's work will be put through the fire to see whether or not it keeps its value. If the work survives the fire, that builder will receive a reward. But if the work is burned up, the builder will suffer great loss. The builders themselves will be saved, but like someone escaping through a wall of flames.

1 Corinthians 3:13–15

No, O people, the LORD has already told you what is good, and this is what he requires: to do what is right, to love mercy, and to walk humbly with your God.

Micah 6:8

. . .

O most merciful Redeemer,
Friend, and Brother,
May we know thee more clearly,
Love thee more dearly,
Follow thee more nearly:
For ever and ever.

Richard of Chichester

. . .

Never let loyalty and kindness get away from you! Wear them like a necklace; write them deep within your heart. Then you will find favor with both God and people, and you will gain a good reputation.

Proverbs 3:3–4

Trust in the LORD with all your heart; do not depend on your own understanding. Seek his will in all you do, and he will direct your paths.

Proverbs 3:5–6

Love each other with genuine affection, and take delight in honoring each other. Never be lazy in your work, but serve the Lord enthusiastically.

Be glad for all God is planning for you. Be patient in trouble, and always be prayerful. When God's children are in need, be the one to help them out. And get into the habit of inviting guests home for dinner or, if they need lodging, for the night.

Romans 12:10–13

Continue to love each other with true Christian love. Don't forget to show hospitality to strangers, for some who have done this have entertained angels without realizing it!

Hebrews 13:1–2

Oh, the joys of those who do not follow the advice of the wicked, or stand around with sinners, or join in with scoffers. But they delight in doing everything the LORD wants; day and night they think about his law. They are like trees planted along the riverbank, bearing fruit each season without fail. Their leaves never wither, and in all they do, they prosper.

Psalm 1:1–3

Or don't you know that your body is the temple of the Holy Spirit, who lives in you and was given to you by God? You do not belong to yourself, for God bought you with a high price. So you must honor God with your body.

1 Corinthians 6:19–20

God wants you to be holy, so you should keep clear of all sexual sin. Then each of you will control your body and live in holiness and honor.

I Thessalonians 4:3–4

. . .

I used to ask God to help me.
Then I asked if I might help him.
I ended up by asking him
to do his work through me.

James Hudson Taylor

. . .

God will bring ruin upon anyone who ruins this temple. For God's temple is holy, and you Christians are that temple. Stop fooling yourselves.

I Corinthians 3:17–18

Here is my final conclusion: Fear God and obey his commands, for this is the duty of every person. God will judge us for everything we do, including every secret thing, whether good or bad.

Ecclesiastes 12:13–14

Remember, it is a sin to know what you ought to do and then not do it.

James 4:17

An elder must be well thought of for his good life. He must be faithful to his wife, and his children must be believers who are not wild or rebellious. An elder must live a blameless life because he is God's minister. He must not be arrogant or quick-tempered; he must not be a heavy drinker, violent, or greedy for money. He must enjoy having guests in his home and must love all that is good. He must live wisely and be fair. He must live a devout and disciplined life. He must have a strong and steadfast belief in the trustworthy message he was taught; then he will be able to encourage others with right teaching and show those who oppose it where they are wrong.

Everything is pure to those whose hearts are pure. But nothing is pure to those who are corrupt and unbelieving, because their minds and consciences are defiled. Such people claim they know God, but they deny him by the way they live. They are despicable and disobedient, worthless for doing anything good.

Titus 1:6, 7–9, 15–16

For God is working in you, giving you the desire to obey him and the power to do what pleases him. As God's partners, we beg you not to reject this marvelous message of God's great kindness. In everything we do we try to show that we are true ministers of God. We patiently endure troubles and hardships and calamities of every kind. We have proved ourselves by our purity, our understanding, our patience, our kindness, our sincere love, and the power of the Holy Spirit. We have faithfully preached the truth. God's power has been working in us. We have righteousness as our weapon, both to attack and to defend ourselves.

Philippians 2:13; 2 Corinthians 6:1, 4, 6–7

A Christian should always remember
that the value of his good works
is not based on their number and excellence,
but on the love of God
which prompts him to do these things.

—John of the Cross

"I command you to love each other in the same way that I love you. And here is how to measure it—the greatest love is shown when people lay down their lives for their friends. You are my friends if you obey me. I no longer call you servants, because a master doesn't confide in his servants. Now you are my friends, since I have told you everything the Father told me."

John 15:12–15

When people do not accept divine guidance, they run wild. But whoever obeys the law is happy.

Proverbs 29:18

Happy is the person who finds wisdom and gains understanding. For the profit of wisdom is better than silver, and her wages are better than gold. But the wisdom that comes from heaven is first of all pure. It is also peace loving, gentle at all times, and willing to yield to others. It is full of mercy and good deeds. It shows no partiality and is always sincere.

Proverbs 3:13–14; James 3:17

A king rejoices in servants who know what they are doing, he is angry with those who cause trouble.

Proverbs 14:35

But I assure you of this: If you ever forget the LORD your God and follow other gods, worshiping and bowing down to them, you will certainly be destroyed.

Deuteronomy 8:19

Stop fooling yourselves. If you think you are wise by this world's standards, you will have to become a fool so you can become wise by God's standards. For the wisdom of this world is foolishness to God. As the Scriptures say, "God catches those who think they are wise in their own cleverness." And again, "The LORD knows the thoughts of the wise, that they are worthless." So don't take pride in following a particular leader. Everything belongs to you. And you belong to Christ, and Christ belongs to God.

I Corinthians 3:18–21, 23

. . .

Teach us to care and not to care;
Teach us to sit still;
Even among these rocks,
Our peace is his will.

T. S. Eliot

. . .

But if you are unwilling to serve the LORD, then choose today whom you will serve. . . . But as for me and my family, we will serve the Lord. The people replied, "We would never forsake the LORD and worship other gods. As for me, I will certainly not sin against the LORD by ending my prayers for you. And I will continue to teach you what is good and right. But be sure to fear the LORD and sincerely worship him. Think of all the wonderful things he has done for you.

Joshua 24:15–16; I Samuel 12:23–24

Obey the government, for God is the one who put it there. All governments have been placed in power by God. So those who refuse to obey the laws of the land are refusing to obey God, and punishment will follow.

Romans 13:1–2

Remember your leaders who first taught you the word of God. Think of all the good that has come from their lives, and trust the Lord as they do. So do not be attracted by strange, new ideas. Your spiritual strength comes from God's special favor, not from ceremonial rules about food, which don't help those who follow them. Obey your spiritual leaders and do what they say. Their work is to watch over your souls, and they know they are accountable to God. Give them reason to do this joyfully and not with sorrow. That would certainly not be for your benefit.

Hebrews 13:7, 9, 17

Elders who do their work well should be paid well, especially those who work hard at both preaching and teaching. He must manage his own family well, with children who respect and obey him. For if a man cannot manage his own household, how can he take care of God's church?

1 Timothy 5:17; 3:4–5

Slaves, obey your earthly masters with deep respect and fear. Serve them sincerely as you would serve Christ. Work hard, but not just to please your masters when they are watching. As slaves of Christ, do the will of God with all your heart. Work with enthusiasm, as though you were working for the Lord rather than for people.

Ephesians 6:5–7

. . .

As a blind man has no idea of colors,
so have we no idea of the manner
by which the all-wise God
perceives and understands all things.

Sir Isaac Newton

. . .

Dear brothers and sisters, honor those who are your leaders in the Lord's work. They work hard among you and warn you against all that is wrong. Think highly of them and give them your wholehearted love because of their work. And remember to live peaceably with each other.

Brothers and sisters, we urge you to warn those who are lazy. Encourage those who are timid. Take tender care of those who are weak. Be patient with everyone.

See that no one pays back evil for evil, but always try to do good to each other and to everyone else. Keep away from every kind of evil. Now may the God of peace make you holy in every way, and may your whole spirit and soul and body be kept blameless until that day when our Lord Jesus Christ comes again.

I Thessalonians 5:12–15, 22, 23

Household

Unless the LORD builds a house, the work of the builders is useless. Be glad: rejoice forever in my creation!

Psalm 127:1; Isaiah 65:18

For God has said, "I will never fail you. I will never forsake you." Don't be afraid, for I am with you. Do not be dismayed, for I am your God. I will strengthen you. I will help you. I will uphold you with my victorious right hand.

Hebrews 13:5; Isaiah 41:10

The curse of the LORD is on the house of the wicked, but his blessing is on the home of the upright. There is treasure in the house of the godly, but the earnings of the wicked bring trouble. It is better to have little with fear for the LORD than to have great treasure with turmoil.

Proverbs 3:33; 15:6; 15:16

So honor the LORD and serve him wholeheartedly. . . . Then choose today whom you will serve. . . . But as for me and my family, we will serve the LORD. The people replied, "We would never forsake the LORD and worship other gods."

Joshua 24:14–16

How happy are those who fear the LORD—all who follow his ways! You will enjoy the fruit of your labor. How happy you will be! How rich your life! Your wife will be like a fruitful vine, flourishing within your home. And look at all those children! There they sit around your table as vigorous and healthy as young olive trees. That is the LORD's reward for those who fear him.

Psalm 128:1–4

. . .

I am sorry for men who
do not read the Bible every day.
I wonder why they deprive themselves of
the strength and the pleasure.

Woodrow Wilson

. . .

It will not be like the past, when invaders took the houses and confiscated the vineyards. For my people will live as long as trees and will have time to enjoy their hard-won gains. They will not work in vain, and their children will not be doomed to misfortune. For they are people blessed by the LORD, and their children, too, will be blessed. I will answer them before they even call to me. While they are still talking to me about their needs, I will go ahead and answer their prayers!

Isaiah 65:22–24

I will continue this everlasting covenant between us, generation after generation. It will continue between me and your offspring forever. And I will always be your God and the God of your descendants after you.

Genesis 17:7

Work hard so God can approve you. Be a good worker, one who does not need to be ashamed and who correctly explains the word of truth. So get rid of all the filth and evil in your lives, and humbly accept the message God has planted in your hearts, for it is strong enough to save your souls.

And remember, it is a message to obey, not just to listen to. If you don't obey, you are only fooling yourself.

2 Timothy 2:15; James 1:21–22

"Anyone who listens to my teaching and obeys me is wise, like a person who builds a house on solid rock. Though the rain comes in torrents and the floodwaters rise and the winds beat against that house, it won't collapse, because it is built on rock. But anyone who hears my teaching and ignores it is foolish, like a person who builds a house on sand. When the rains and floods come and the winds beat against that house, it will fall with a mighty crash."

Matthew 7:24–27

"Any kingdom at war with itself is doomed. A city or home divided against itself is doomed."

Matthew 12:25

This should be your ambition: to live a quiet life, minding your own business and working with your hands, just as we commanded you before. As a result, people who are not Christians will respect the way you live, and you will not need to depend on others to meet your financial needs.

I Thessalonians 4:11–12

. . .

[In the Bible are found]
shallows where a lamb could wade
and depths where an elephant could drown.

Matthew Henry

. . .

Marriage

Now about the questions you asked in your letter. Yes, it is good to live a celibate life. But because there is so much sexual immorality, each man should have his own wife, and each woman should have her own husband.

I Corinthians 7:1–2

Now I say to those who aren't married and to widows—it's better to stay unmarried, just as I am. But if they can't control themselves, they should go ahead and marry. It's better to marry than to burn with lust.

I Corinthians 7:8–9

In everything you do, I want you to be free from the concerns of this life. An unmarried man can spend his time doing the Lord's work and thinking how to please him. But a married man can't do that so well. He has to think about his earthly responsibilities and how to please his wife. His interests are divided. In the same way, a woman who is no longer married or has never been married can be more devoted to the Lord in body and in spirit, while the married woman must be concerned about her earthly responsibilities and how to please her husband.

I Corinthians 7:32–35

So I advise these younger widows to marry again, have children, and take care of their own homes. Then the enemy will not be able to say anything against them. For I am afraid that some of them have already gone astray and now follow Satan.

I Timothy 5:14–15

The man who finds a wife finds a treasure and receives Jesus Christ, through who God made everything and through whom we have been given life. But there is one thing I want you to know. A man is responsible to Christ, a woman is responsible to her husband, and Christ is responsible to God.

Proverbs 18:22; I Corinthians 11:3

For a husband is the head of his wife as Christ is the head of his body, the church; he gave his life to be her Savior. As the church submits to Christ, so you wives must submit to your husbands in everything.

Ephesians 5:23–24

A man should not wear anything on his head when worshiping, for man is God's glory, made in God's own image, but woman is the glory of man. And man was not made for woman's benefit, but woman was made for man. But in relationships among the Lord's people, women are not independent of men, and men are not independent of women. For although the first woman came from man, all men have been born from women ever since, and everything comes from God.

I Corinthians 11:7, 9; 11–12

And you husbands must love your wives with the same love Christ showed the church. He gave up his life for her. In the same way, husbands ought to love their wives as they love their own bodies. For a man is actually loving himself when he loves his wife. And we are his body. As the Scriptures say, "A man leaves his father and mother and is joined to his wife, and the two are united into one." This is a great mystery, but it is an illustration of the way Christ and the church are one. So again I say, each man must love his wife as he loves himself, and the wife must respect her husband.

Ephesians 5:25, 28, 30–33

"Haven't you read the Scriptures?" Jesus replied. "They record that from the beginning 'God made them male and female.' And he said, "This explains why a man leaves his father and mother and is joined to his wife, and the two are united into one.' Since they are no longer two but one, let no one separate them, for God has joined them together."

Matthew 19:4–6

You wives will submit to your husbands as you do to the Lord. For a husband is the head of his wife as Christ is the head of his body, the church; he gave his life to be her Savior.

Ephesians 5:22–23

. . .

A successful marriage is not a gift; it is an achievement.

Ann Landers

. . .

The husband should not deprive his wife of sexual intimacy, which is her right as a married woman, nor should the wife deprive her husband. The wife gives authority over her body to her husband, and the husband also gives authority over his body to his wife. So do not deprive each other of sexual relations. The only exception to this rule would be the agreement of both husband and wife to refrain from sexual intimacy for a limited time, so they can give themselves more completely to prayer. Afterward they should come together again so that Satan won't be able to tempt them because of their lack of self-control.

I Corinthians 7:3–5

Give honor to marriage, and remain faithful to one another in marriage. God will surely judge people who are immoral and those who commit adultery.

Hebrews 13:4

"You have heard that the law of Moses says, 'Do not commit adultery.' But I say, anyone who even looks at a woman with lust in his eye has already committed adultery with her in his heart."

Matthew 5:27–28

. . .

You will never see perfection in your mate,
nor will he or she find it in you.

James C. Dobson

. . .

In the same way, you wives must accept the authority of your husbands, even those who refuse to accept the Good News. Your godly lives will speak to them better than any words. In the same way, you husbands must give honor to your wives. Treat her with understanding as you live together. She may be weaker than you are, but she is your equal partner in God's gift of new life. If you don't treat her as you should, your prayers will not be heard.

Finally, all of you should be of one mind, full of sympathy toward each other, loving one another with tender hearts and humble minds. Instead, you must worship Christ as Lord of your life. And if you are asked about your Christian hope, always be ready to explain it.

I Peter 3:1, 7–8, 15

Now, I will speak to the rest of you, though I do not have a direct command from the Lord. If a Christian man has a wife who is an unbeliever and she is willing to continue living with him, he must not leave her. And if a Christian woman has a husband who is an unbeliever, and he is willing to continue living with her, she must not leave him. For the Christian wife brings holiness to her marriage, and the Christian husband brings holiness to his marriage. Otherwise, your children would not have a godly influence, but now they are set apart for him. (But if the husband or wife who isn't a Christian insists on leaving, let them go. In such cases the Christian husband or wife is not required to stay with them, for God wants his children to live in peace.) You wives must remember that your husbands might be converted because of you. And you husbands must remember that your wives might be converted because of you.

I Corinthians 7:12–16

Now, for those who are married, I have a command that comes not from me, but from the Lord. A wife must not leave her husband. But if she does leave him, let her remain single or else go back to him. And the husband must not leave his wife. A wife is married to her husband as long as he lives. If her husband dies, she is free to marry whomever she wishes, but this must be a marriage acceptable to the Lord.

I Corinthians 7:10–11; 39

"You have heard that the law of Moses says, 'A man can divorce his wife by merely giving her a letter of divorce.' But I say that a man who divorces his wife, unless she has been unfaithful, causes her to commit adultery. And anyone who marries a divorced woman commits adultery. And if a woman divorces her husband and remarries, she commits adultery."

Matthew 5:31–32; Mark 10:12

. . .

Success in marriage is more than
finding the right person:
it is being the right person.

Robert Browning

. . .

Family

"And this is my covenant with them," says the LORD. "My Spirit will not leave them, and neither will these words I have given you. They will be on your lips and on the lips of your children and your children's children forever. I, the LORD, have spoken!"

Isaiah 59:21

My child, never forget the things I have taught you. Store my commands in your heart, for they will give you a long and satisfying life. Never let loyalty and kindness get away from you! Wear them like a necklace; write them deep within your heart. Then you will find favor with both God and people, and you will gain a good reputation.

Proverbs 3:1–4

So put away all falsehood and "tell your neighbor the truth" because we belong to each other. And "don't sin by letting anger gain control over you." Don't let the sun go down while you are still angry, for anger gives a mighty foothold to the Devil. A gentle answer turns away wrath, but harsh words stir up anger.

Ephesians 4:25–27; Proverbs 15:1

And now a word to you fathers. Don't make your children angry by the way you treat them. Rather, bring them up with the discipline and instruction approved by the Lord. Your anger can never make things right in God's sight. Fathers, don't aggravate your children. If you do, they will become discouraged and quit trying.

Ephesians 6:4; James 1:20; Colossians 3:21

Grandchildren are the crowning glory of the aged; parents are the pride of their children. Good people leave an inheritance to their grandchildren, but the sinner's wealth passes to the godly.

Proverbs 17:6; 13:22

Children are a gift from the LORD; they are a reward from him. I will teach all your citizens, and their prosperity will be great. You will live under a government that is just and fair. Your enemies will stay far away; you will live in peace. You will live under a government that is just and fair. Your enemies will stay far away; you will live in peace. Terror will not come near.

Psalm 127:3; Isaiah 54:13–14

. . .

*A family is
a place where principles are hammered
and honed on the anvil of everyday living.*

Charles Swindoll

. . .

Teach your children to choose the right path, and when they are older, they will remain upon it. Discipline your children, and they will give you happiness and peace of mind.

Proverbs 22:6; 29:17

Sensible children bring joy to their father; foolish children despise their mother. Only a fool despises a parent's discipline; whoever learns from correction is wise.

Proverbs 15:20, 5

Discipline your children while there is hope. If you don't, you will ruin their lives. Don't fail to correct your children. They won't die if you spank them. Physical discipline may well save them from death. If you refuse to discipline your children, it proves you don't love them; if you love your children, you will be prompt to discipline them. A youngster's heart is filled with foolishness, but discipline will drive it away. To discipline and reprimand a child produces wisdom, but a mother is disgraced by an undisciplined child.

Proverbs 19:18; 23:13–14; 13:24; 22:15; 29:15

My child, how I will rejoice if you become wise. My child, listen and be wise. Keep your heart on the right course. Listen to your father, who gave you life, and don't despise your mother's experience when she is old. The father of godly children has cause for joy. What a pleasure it is to have wise children. So give your parents joy. May she who gave you birth be happy. O my son, give me your heart. May your eyes delight in my ways of wisdom.

Proverbs 23:15, 19, 22, 24–26

Children, obey your parents because you belong to the Lord, for this is the right thing to do. "Honor your father and mother." This is the first of the Ten Commandments that ends with a promise. And this is the promise: If you honor your father and mother, "you will live a long life, full of blessing." You children must always obey your parents, for this is what pleases the Lord.

Ephesians 6:1–3; Colossians 3:20

Listen, my child, to what your father teaches you. Don't neglect your mother's teachings. What you learn from them will crown you with grace and clothe you with honor.

Proverbs 1:8–9

. . .

I believe the family was
established long before
the church,
and my duty is
to my family first.
I am not to neglect my family.

D. L. Moody

. . .

My son, obey your father's commands, and don't neglect your mother's teaching. Keep their words always in your heart. Tie them around your neck. Wherever you walk, their counsel can lead you. When you sleep, they will protect you. When you wake up in the morning, they will advise you. For these commands and this teaching are a lamp to light the way ahead of you. The correction of discipline is the way of life.

Proverbs 6:20–23

I command you—be strong and courageous! Do not be afraid or discouraged. For the LORD your God is with you wherever you go.

Joshua 1:9

Never speak harshly to an older man, but appeal to him respectfully as though he were your own father. Talk to the younger men as you would to your own brothers. Treat the older women as you would your mother, and treat the younger women with all purity as your own sisters.

1 Timothy 5:1–2

Trust in the LORD with all your heart; do not depend on your own understanding. Don't lose sight of my words for they bring life and radiant health to anyone who discovers their meaning.

Proverbs 3:5; 4:21–22

All who are victorious will inherit all these blessings, and I will be their God, and they will be my children.

Revelation 21:7

A Virtuous Woman

Who can find a virtuous and capable wife? She is worth more than precious rubies. Her husband can trust her, and she will greatly enrich his life. She will not hinder him but help him all her life.

She gets up before dawn to prepare breakfast for her household and plan the day's work for her servant girls.

She is energentic and strong, a hard worker.

She extends a helping hand to the poor and opens her arms to the needy.

She is clothed with strength and dignity, and she laughs with no fear of the future. When she speaks, her words are wise, and kindness is the rule when she gives instructions. She carefully watches all that goes on in her household and does not have to bear the consequences of laziness.

Her children stand and bless her. Her husband praises her. "There are many virtuous and capable women in the world, but you surpass them all!"

Charm is deceptive, and beauty does not last; but a woman who fears the LORD will be greatly praised. Reward her for all she has done. Let her deeds publicly declare her praise.

Proverbs 31:10–12, 15, 17, 20, 25–31

A wise women builds her house; a foolish woman tears hers down with her own hands.

The house of the wicked will perish, but the tent of the godly will flourish.

Proverbs 14:1, 11

How are our churches beautified,
our sick tended, our poor fed,
our children taught and cared for and civilized?
Do you think the masculine element goes
for much in these things?
No, . . .women are the church's strong rock.
As they were the last at the foot of the cross,
so they have become the first at the altar.

—Mary Elizabeth Braddon

Awake

I hope that the day is near at hand
when the advent of
the great God will appear,
for all things everywhere are
boiling, burning, moving,
falling, sinking, groaning.

—Martin Luther

"And since you don't know when they will happen stay alert and keep watch. So keep a sharp lookout! For you do not know when the homeowner will return—at evening, midnight, early dawn, or late daybreak. Don't let him find you sleeping when he arrives without warning. What I say to you I say to everyone: Watch for his return!"

Mark 13:33, 35–37

But you, lazybones, how long will you sleep? When will you wake up? I want you to learn this lesson: A little extra sleep, a little more slumber, a little folding of the hands to rest—and poverty will pounce on you like a bandit; scarcity will attack you like an armed robber.

Proverbs 6:9–11

"No one knows the day or hour when these things will happen, not even the angels in heaven or the Son himself. Only the Father knows."

Mark 13:32

"Let your good deeds shine out for all to see, so that everyone will praise your heavenly Father."

Matthew 5:16

Arise! Let your light shine for all the nations to see! For the glory of the LORD is shining upon you. Darkness as black as night will cover all the nations of the earth, but the glory of the Lord will shine over you.

Isaiah 60:1–2

Another reason for right living is that you know how late it is; time is running out. Wake up, for the coming of our salvation is nearer now than when we first believed. The night is almost gone; the day of salvation will soon be here. So don't live in darkness. Get rid of your evil deeds. Shed them like dirty clothes. Clothe yourselves with the armor of right living, as those who live in the light. We should be decent and true in everything we do, so that everyone can approve of our behavior. Don't participate in wild parties and getting drunk, or in adultery and immoral living, or in fighting and jealousy. But let the Lord Jesus Christ take control of you, and don't think of ways to indulge your evil desires.

Romans 13:11–14

. . .

We are not a post-war generation;
but a pre-peace generation.
Jesus is coming.

Corrie ten Boom

. . .

"Watch out! Don't let me find you living in careless ease and drunkenness, and filled with the worries of this life. Don't let that day catch you unaware, as in a trap. For that day will come upon everyone living on the earth. Keep a constant watch. And pray that, if possible, you may escape these horrors and stand before the Son of Man."

Luke 21:34–36

"I have come as a light to shine in this dark world, so that all who put their trust in me will no longer remain in the darkness."

John 12:46

The people who walk in darkness will see a great light—a light that will shine on all who live in the land where death casts its shadow.

Isaiah 9:2

Twenty-third Psalm

NEW LIVING TRANSLATION

The Twenty-third Psalm is
the nightingale of the psalms.
It is small, of a homely feather,
singing shyly out of obscurity;
but it has filled the air of the whole world
with melodious joy.

—Henry Ward Beecher

The Lord is my shepherd:
  I have everything I need.
He lets me rest in green meadows;
  he leads me beside peaceful streams.
He renews my strength.
  He guides me along right paths,
    bringing honor to his name.
Even when I walk through
  the dark valley of death,
I will not be afraid,
  for you are close beside me.
Your rod and your staff
  protect and comfort me.

You prepare a feast for me
in the presence of my enemies.
You welcome me as a guest,
anointing my head with oil.
My cup overflows with blessings.

Surely your goodness and unfailing love
will pursue me all the days of my life,
and I will live in the house
of the Lord forever.

—Psalm 23